COL

D0353322

WILD
FLOWERS
PHOTOGUIDE

Text by Martin Walters
Photographic Consultants
David and Jean Hosking

HarperCollins*Publishers*

HarperCollins*Publishers*
PO Box, Glasgow G4 0NB
First published 1994

Reprint 9 8 7 6 5 4 3 2

Typeset by TJ Graphics

Printed in Italy by Amadeus S.p.A.

CONTENTS KEY

The species in this book fall roughly into 21 different flower shapes. You should be able to match the flower shape of the species you are trying to identify to one of the drawings below, to find out to which family it belongs. Once you have looked up the right family section, you should be able to find your species. Some flower shapes are distinctive and characteristic of one family only. Others, eg regular flowers with 5 petals, appear in several families, and the key will direct you to all of these. The family name and a sketch of the flower shape appear at the top of each species entry page.

BUTTERCUP FAMILY p.13, 14, 19
WATER-LILY FAMILY p.21, 22
PRIMROSE FAMILY p.135
GENTIAN FAMILY p.139

MIGNONETTE FAMILY p.40
PEA FAMILY p.77, 82
ROSE FAMILY p.94
STONECROP FAMILY p.98
LOOSESTRIFE FAMILY p.101
WILLOW-HERB FAMILY p.104, 105
SPURGE FAMILY p.124
PRIMROSE FAMILY p.134
BOGBEAN FAMILY p.141
BORAGE FAMILY p.146
FIGWORT FAMILY p.155, 158, 168, 171
MINT FAMILY p.185, 187
DAISY FAMILY p.216, 218, 220
ORCHID FAMILY p.247-251

BUTTERCUP FAMILY p.15, 20
CABBAGE FAMILY p.30
ROSE FAMILY p.87, 95
SEA-LAVENDER FAMILY p.128, 129
MINT FAMILY p.172-175, 178
BEDSTRAW FAMILY p.195-200
VALERIAN FAMILY p.202, 203
DAISY FAMILY p.209, 217
LILY FAMILY p.241, 243

PEA FAMILY p.76, 78-80
ROSE FAMILY p.96
BELLFLOWER FAMILY p.193
TEASEL FAMILY p.204-207
DAISY FAMILY p.210, 214, 224-229

DAISY FAMILY p.208, 211-213, 215, 219, 221-223,
230-239

CARROT FAMILY p.106-120

BINDWEED FAMILY p.147-150

NIGHTSHADE FAMILY p.153, 154
BELLFLOWER FAMILY p.189-192
LILY FAMILY p.240,242
DAFFODIL FAMILY p.245

FUMITORY FAMILY p.27, 28
BORAGE FAMILY p.142, 143
FIGWORT FAMILY p.167, 169
HONEYSUCKLE FAMILY p.201

MILKWORT FAMILY p.47

PEA FAMILY p.75, 81, 83-86

MINT FAMILY p.176, 177, 179-184, 186, 188

VIOLET FAMILY p.41-46
BALSAM FAMILY p.74
FIGWORT FAMILY p.156, 157

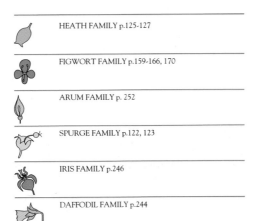

INTRODUCTION

This book will help you identify the most common wildflowers of Britain and Ireland. There are about 1500 species of wildflower in these islands. The 288 in this book are those most likely to be seen during a walk in the countryside, be it on the coast or in the mountains, woodlands, hedgerows, fields or wetlands. **All those terms printed in bold in the species entries will be explained in this introduction.**

What is a wildflower?

Wildflowers are those flowers which grow naturally in our countryside. Many are **native** – they form part of the original flora and have not been **introduced** by people. Others have been introduced either deliberately or via gardens (**garden escapes**) or farms. Many cultivated plants grown for food or medicine are descended from **ancestors** which still grow wild today (eg Wild Carrot, p.119). Some wildflowers are called 'weeds' simply when they grow where they are not wanted, usually in gardens or fields. They can be very pretty.

The flower

A typical flower has a ring of **petals** which make up the **corolla**. Often brightly coloured, they give the flower its main colour. Some species have a tube-like extension or **spur** at the back of the flower. Below the petals is another ring or **calyx** of petal-like **sepals** which protect the flower when it is in bud. Although usually green or brown, some sepals are brightly coloured. Outside the sepals there may be special leaves or **bracts** which also protect the flower.

At the centre of a flower there is usually a tall column or

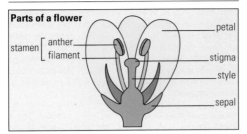

Parts of a flower

stamen [anther
         filament

petal

stigma

style

sepal

style, topped by the sometimes feathery **stigma** – this is the female part and is where the **pollen** (the male reproductive cells) from a male flower lands during pollination (the first stage in reproduction). The male parts are the **stamens** which each consist of a tall, thin stalk or **filament**, with an enlarged part called the **anther** at the top containing the pollen. Not all flowers are both male and female, some are single sex only.

A shoot may have a single flower at its tip, but more often there are several flowers arranged in a number of different ways. If the group of flowers is tightly packed, it may be called a **flowerhead**. Sometimes (see Daisy Family) the flowerhead may look like a single flower, but is actually made up of many tiny flowers or **florets** which which may look like the single petal of a normal flower. These petal-like florets are **ray florets**, those florets at the centre of the Daisy flower are **tube** or **disc florets**. A **spike** is a flowerhead in which all the flowers are attached to a single column. The flowers of the Carrot Family (**umbellifers**) grow in an arrangement known as an **umbel** – many flowers arise from the same point on the stalk, to form a flat-topped umbrella shape. In Lords-and-ladies (p.252), each 'flower' is in fact the central rod (extended stem) or **spadix**, enclosed by a translucent hood or **spathe**. The actual flowers are tiny and grow at the base of the spadix.

The stem

The **stem** is the main above-ground part of a plant, and normally grows upwards. There are many different kinds of stem. **Rhizomes** are underground stems. **Runners** grow horizontally above or below the ground and develop small roots and new plants at their tips. Some parts of the stem or leaf may develop **tendrils**, which aid climbing plants. **Bulbs** are undergound stems, with compressed, fleshy leaves, from which flowers such as Daffodils grow up quickly in the spring. **Bulbils** are tiny bulbs which fall off the parent plant, and grow into new plants the next season. Some species, such as many thistles, have stems which are flattened at the edges (**winged** stems).

The leaf

Leaves grow out from the sides of the plant, from thickened parts of the stem called **nodes**. They may grow **opposite** each other, or be **alternate** up the stem. When several leaves grow round the stem at each node, they are described as **whorled** or in **whorls**. Leaves growing at the bottom of the stem are called **base** or **basal** leaves. When these all spread from the centre they are known as a **rosette**. Those higher up are called **stem leaves**. The angle where the leaf stem joins the main stem is called the **axil**. **Bracts** are leaves growing close to a flower or flowerhead and protecting it. Sometimes leaf-like **stipules** grow at the base of a leafstalk.

A leaf consists of the leafstalk or **petiole**, and the **blade** which has a number of **veins**, including a central vein or **midrib**. **Simple** leaves have an undivided blade, while **compound** leaves are made up of separate **leaflets**. When these grow from the same point, like the fingers of a hand, the leaf is described as **palmate**. When they grow along either side, the leaf is **pinnate**.

Leaves can be a number of different shapes, including: **linear** (long and narrow), **lanceolate (**tapering like the blade of a lance), **oval**, **oblong**, **triangular**, **spoon-shaped**, **kidney-shaped**, **heart-shaped**, **trifoliate** (like a clover leaf), **spear-shaped**, **arrow-shaped**. Leaves may have smooth edges, or they may be **toothed** or **lobed**.

The fruit

The fruit develops in the flower after pollination, and protects the seeds until they are ripe. There are many different fruit types: some are fleshy and edible, and eaten by birds and other animals; others are hooked and cling to fur or clothing; and others are **pods** or **capsules** which release seeds when dry.

Danger and Conservation

Although culinary and medicinal uses of plants are given in this book, many species are **poisonous** (some, eg Hemlock, very poisonous), including many used in herbal medicine. **Do not eat any wild plant or prepare and use your own natural**

medicines. Do not pick or uproot any wild flower – many are rare and specially protected. No wildflower may be uprooted without permission.

How to identify wildflowers

If you know the name of a wildflower you can simply look it up in the **index** of common names at the back of the book. Closely related flowers belong to the same **family**. If you cannot identify a flower, but think it is related to one you *do* recognise, then look up the one you know and look through the species in its family (the family name appears at the top of each page). It is likely that your new find will be in that section. If you have no idea what your flower is, use the symbols in the **contents pages** (pp. 3-6) to decide what kind of flower shape it has. Then look through the families which contain flowers of that shape. The flower shape of each species appears at the top of each species entry page. Many families have a distinctive flower shape (eg the Bindweed Family). Others (eg the Daisy Family) contain species with different flower shapes, and thus have more than one characteristic shape.

Flower names

The **common (English) names** of flowers vary, but for most there is a recommended name which we have used. Well-known alternatives are also listed. Many names are very old and derived from traditional medicinal or culinary uses of the plant. Where these origins are known, we have given them. Every species also has a unique **scientific (Latin) name**, which is unvarying and international. It is always italicised and in two parts (binomial): the **genus** name is written first, with an initial capital letter, followed by the specific name eg *Viola lutea*. (Each **family** contains one or more genera (singular: genus), a genus being a group of similar **species**.)

Species entries

The first paragraph provides a general description of the plant (climber, shrub, etc), with notes on the size, colour and shape of its leaves and flowers. For most flowers the width of the open flower is given (eg 8 mm across), but for long, narrower flowers, the length is given (eg 8 mm long). Flower colour on its own is not a good guide to identification – many species share colour, and it may vary within a species or with the season. Leaf shapes vary but they can aid identification, when combined with other features.

Size is the average height of the plant. Most grow upright, but some creep along the ground or climb on other plants, in which case the length of the spreading plant is given.

Habitat notes the main type of country where the species grows. Many are typically found in a particular habitat – eg marsh. This information may help confirm identification.

Range gives the area in which the species might be found. Some, for example, only grow in warmer sites in the south, while others are restricted to mountains of the north and west.

Flowers is when to see the species in flower. This aids identification, as similar species may have different flowering periods.

Similar species are those common species which might easily be confused with the main species described.

MARSH MARIGOLD   *Caltha palustris*

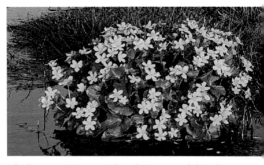

Also known as Kingcup. A large buttercup with big, glossy, deep-green, kidney-shaped leaves. The bright yellow flowers look like giant buttercups and appear in spring and early summer. They are bigger than those of other buttercups, up to 5 cm across when fully opened. Clumps of Marsh Marigolds tend to hug the banks of streams. In late summer produces claw-shaped seed **pods**.

Size	To 50 cm.
Habitat	Grows alongside ditches and streams. Also in marshes and wet woods.
Range	Throughout Britain and Ireland, up to 1000 m.
Flowers	March-July

WOOD ANEMONE *Anemone nemorosa*

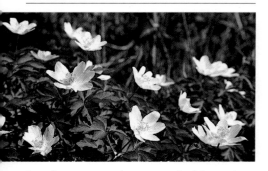

One of our prettiest early spring woodland flowers. Large patches of the woodland floor are sometimes carpeted with this species. It has star-like, 6-petalled white or pinkish flowers set against dark green, three-lobed leaves. The flowers are about 4 cm across.

Size To 30 cm.
Habitat Mainly deciduous woodland. Also hedges and shaded banks.
Range Throughout, but very local in S Ireland.
Flowers March-May

TRAVELLER'S JOY *Clematis vitalba*

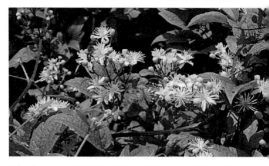

Also known as Old Man's Beard because of its white feathery fruits. Climbs and twines up trees and in hedges. Develops small, creamy-coloured, fragrant flowers, about 2 cm across, which grow in clusters. The leaves usually have five leaflets. The downy fruits develop in September and October. Each fruit or **achene** has a feather-like **style** attached.

Size Stems to 30 m

Habitat Mainly on calcareous soils, often in the shade of trees and thick hedges, and along the margins of woods.

Range Common, but only in southern England, south of the Mersey-Humber line, and in Wales.

Flowers July-August

MEADOW BUTTERCUP *Ranunculus acris*

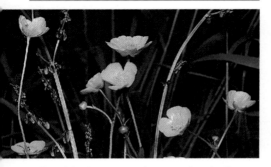

Tallest of the three common buttercups (see also Creeping Buttercup p.17 and Bulbous Buttercup p.18). The **sepals** are cupped around the bright yellow flowers which are 18-25 mm across. Unlike those of the other two buttercups, the flower-stalks are not furrowed. The leaves are lobed and hairy.

Size	To 1 m
Habitat	Damp meadows and pastures. Also found on rocks and ledges in mountains.
Range	Common throughout
Flowers	June-July

CREEPING BUTTERCUP *Ranunculus repens*

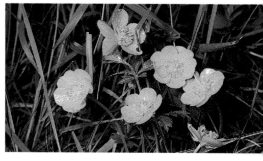

Creeps through grasses by means of long shoots or **runners**. Roots grow from these runners and form new plants which grow in large, often circular, patches. The flowers are 2-3 cm across. The **sepals** encircle the petals and the flower-stalks are furrowed. The leaves are lobed and hairy.

Size	To 60 cm
Habitat	Damp and wet meadows and pastures. Also wet woods, sand dunes and roadsides. Survives mowing, and therefore common on lawns.
Range	Common throughout
Flowers	May-August

BULBOUS BUTTERCUP *Ranunculus bulbosus*

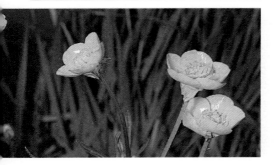

The common name refers to the swollen base of the stem. The plant is best identified by the **sepals**, which turn back from the flower, along the stems. The flowers are 2-3 cm across and the flower stalks are furrowed. The leaves are lobed and usually hairy.

Size	To 45 cm
Habitat	Likes pastures, but avoids damp conditions. Prefers lime-rich soils.
Range	Common throughout England and much of Wales; scattered in Scotland and Ireland.
Flowers	May-June

LESSER CELANDINE *Ranunculus ficaria*

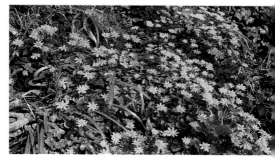

Has bright yellow flowers, 2-3 cm across, each with 8-12 narrow petals and three **sepals**. Flowers fade with age to a creamy white colour. The leaves are rounded and glossy. An ointment for treating piles can be made from the fresh plant, so it is sometimes also called Pilewort.

Size	To 25 cm
Habitat	Native woodland and grassland. Also grows alongside streams and as a garden weed.
Range	Common throughout, but more scattered in S Ireland.
Flowers	March-May

COMMON MEADOW-RUE *Thalictrum flavum*

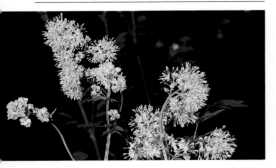

Tall plant with fluffy clusters (about 10 cm across) of tiny yellowish flowers. The yellow colour comes from the long **stamens** which are the most distinctive part of the flowers. The stems are rather firm and furrowed and the leaves divided. Could be confused with Meadowsweet (p.87) when seen from a distance.

Size	To 1 m
Habitat	Wet meadows, marshes and fens. Also river banks.
Range	Scattered in most of England except extreme SW; rarer in Wales and Ireland; virtually unknown in Scotland.
Flowers	July-August

WHITE WATER-LILY *Nymphaea alba*

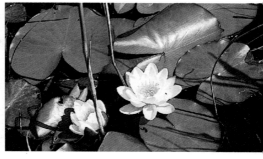

The largest and most showy of waterplants, with big, floating white flowers each with about 20 petals, and up to about 20 cm across. The floating leaves are round in outline and there are no underwater leaves.

Size	Leaves are up to 30 cm across
Habitat	Lakes and ponds
Range	Scattered throughout
Flowers	July-August

YELLOW WATER-LILY *Nuphar lutea*

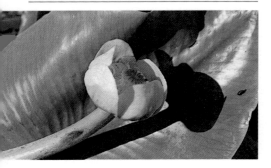

Unlike White Water-lilies (p.21), these flowers stand up on stalks clear of the water surface. The yellow flowers are about 5 cm across and later develop into bottle-shaped fruit **capsules** (hence the alternative name 'Brandy-bottle'). The plant has oval-shaped floating leaves and lettuce-like underwater leaves.

Size Leaves are up to 30 cm long
Habitat Lakes, ponds and slow streams
Range Scattered throughout, but commonest in S.
Flowers June-August

COMMON POPPY *Papaver rhoeas*

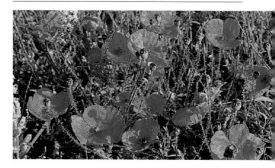

The commonest of our poppies, with large bright scarlet flowers, up to 10 cm across. Each flower has four rather crinkled petals, sometimes with a dark spot near the base. The leaves are deeply divided, with narrow segments. The fruit is a rounded 'pepper-pot' from which seeds are shaken by the wind.

Size To 60 cm

Habitat A weed of cereal crops, especially along field margins which have escaped spraying with weedkillers. Sometimes grows in quantity along newly created road cuttings.

Range Common throughout, but rarer in N and W.

Flowers June-August

LONG-HEADED POPPY *Papaver dubium*

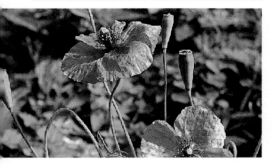

The flowers are sightly smaller, 3-7 cm across, and a paler red than Common Poppies (p.23). The leaves are divided, with shorter and broader segments than those of the Common Poppy. The fruit **capsule** is long, smooth and club-shaped.

Size To 60 cm
Habitat Weed of arable fields and waste places
Range Throughout, including N and W where it is more common than the Common Poppy.
Flowers June-July

YELLOW HORNED-POPPY *Glaucium flavum*

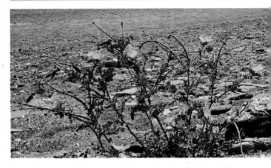

A striking seaside species, this poppy has bright yellow flowers, and long, curved, horn-shaped fruit **pods**. The flowers are 6-9 cm across. Both leaves and stems are a soft blue-grey colour, and the leaves are deeply lobed.

Size	To 80 cm
Habitat	Coastal shingle banks.
Range	All around coasts, but mainly in S and W. N to Argyll and Berwick. Rather rare in Ireland.
Flowers	June-September

POPPY FAMILY

GREATER CELANDINE *Chelidonium majus*

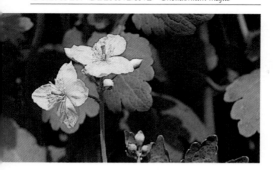

Badly named, as this is not related to the Lesser Celandine, but to the poppies. It has rather brittle stems and grey-green leaves, which exude a poisonous, bright orange sap when broken. The delicate flowers are bright yellow, 2-2.5 cm across and have four petals. The leaves are lobed, and each lobe has coarse teeth. Used in medicine to treat diseases of the gallbladder. Traditionally, the sap was applied to warts.

Size To 1 m
Habitat Common alongside walls, banks and hedgerows. Most often found near houses, as an urban weed.
Range Throughout Britain, but rarer in Scotland; scattered in Ireland.
Flowers May-August

YELLOW CORYDALIS *Corydalis lutea*

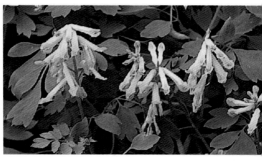

A pretty flower introduced from S Europe and escaped from gardens. Sprouts as clumps of pale green divided leaves from vertical walls in gardens or at the roadside. Each flowering stalk bears a group of up to 10 bright yellow flowers, 12-20 mm long, each with a short **spur**.

Size	To 30 cm
Habitat	Old walls, growing from the mortar between bricks.
Range	Common in England and Wales; local in Scotland and Ireland.
Flowers	May-September

COMMON FUMITORY *Fumaria officinalis*

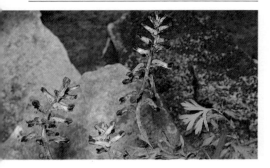

Our most common fumitory, this species has feathery foliage and delicate clusters of up to 20 pink and red flowers, each 7-9 mm long. Used in traditional medicine to treat eczema.

Size	To 40 cm
Habitat	A weed of cultivated land, especially on light soils.
Range	Especially E and central Britain. Scarcer in the W and in Ireland.
Flowers	May-October

CHARLOCK *Sinapis arvensis*

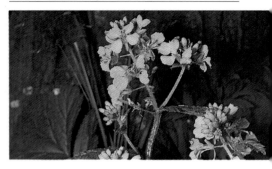

Charlock has heads of bright yellow flowers, each 14-17 mm across. Its leaves are hairy and toothed or lobed. The upper leaves are stalkless and undivided. Its seed **pods** have straight tips, not curved as in the similar White Mustard (*see* below).

Size	To 80 cm
Habitat	A common weed of cereal crops and field margins, especially on chalky or heavy soils. Much reduced by herbicides.
Range	Throughout
Flowers	May-July
Similar species	White Mustard, *Sinapis alba* flowers June-August and has more deeply lobed leaves.

HOARY CRESS *Cardaria draba*

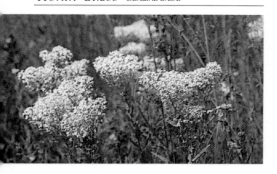

Often obvious on grassy roadsides in late spring as patches of creamy-white **flowerheads**. The individual flowers are about 5 mm across, and their petals twice as long as their **sepals**. The leaves are oval and toothed. Fruits are heart-shaped seed **pods**.

Size To 1 m, but often smaller at roadsides.
Habitat Introduced and now well established on roadsides and as an arable weed.
Range Commonest in S and E. Rarer in Scotland and Ireland.
Flowers May-June

FIELD PENNY-CRESS *Thlaspi arvense*

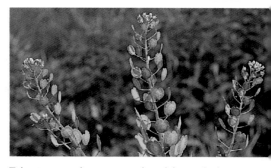

Takes its name from its coin-shaped fruits which are flattened and almost circular, 12-20 mm across. The white flowers are very small (about 5 mm across). Smells unpleasant when crushed. The leaves are **lanceolate**.

Size	To 60 cm
Habitat	A weed of waste ground and arable fields.
Range	Much of England, but reduced by herbicides. Rarer in Wales, Scotland and Ireland.
Flowers	May-July

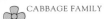 CABBAGE FAMILY

SHEPHERD'S-PURSE *Capsella bursa-pastoris*

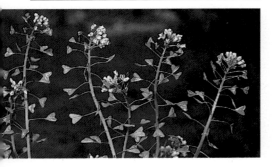

This small weed is best identified by its heart-shaped fruits. These are nearly always present throughout the year, and give the plant its common name (they are shaped like the purses shepherds used to carry). The flowers are white and about 2.5 mm across. The base leaves are oblong in outline and grow as a **rosette** at ground level.

Size To 40 cm
Habitat Weed of waste and cultivated ground.
Range Common throughout
Flowers January-December

COMMON SCURVYGRASS *Cochlearia officinalis*

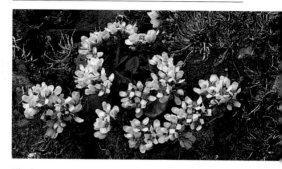

The leaves are succulent, like those of many seaside plants, and heart-shaped. They are a source of Vitamin C and were used by sailors to prevent the disease known as scurvy. The plant is very variable in size. The flowers are about 8-10 mm across, with white (sometimes pink) petals. The fruits are rounded pea-shaped seed **pods**.

Size To 50 cm
Habitat Coastal, on sea walls and banks, and in saltmarshes. Some forms also found inland, on mountain cliffs, streams and spoil-heaps.
Range All around coasts
Flowers May-August

CUCKOOFLOWER *Cardamine pratensis*

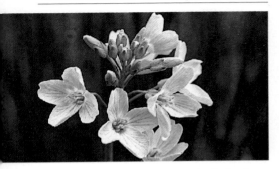

Starts to flower about the same time as the Cuckoo begins to call, hence the common name. Also known as Milkmaids and Lady's Smock. The flowers are pale lilac (sometimes white), up to 2 cm across and have petals about three times as long as the **sepals**. The leaves are **pinnate**, like those of watercress. Often flowers in large patches in marshy areas.

Size	To 60 cm
Habitat	Damp meadows, pastures and along the banks of streams
Range	Common throughout
Flowers	April-June

HAIRY BITTER-CRESS *Cardamine hirsuta*

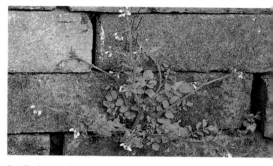

Small plant with a **rosette** of leaves near to the ground.
Flowers are white, about 4 mm across, and the petals are
twice the length of the **sepals**. The leaves have rounded or
oval leaflets. Bitter-cresses are edible and add a sharp
flavour to salads.

Size	To 30 cm
Habitat	Garden weed, also found on bare ground such as scree slopes, walls and rocks.
Range	Common throughout
Flowers	April-August
Similar species	Wavy Bitter-cress, *Cardamine flexuosa*, is larger, with more zig-zag-shaped stems. Common in damp places. April-August.

WINTER-CRESS *Barbarea vulgaris*

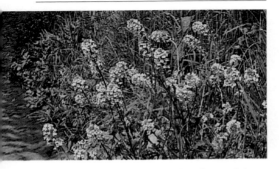

Winter-cress has small bright yellow flowers, 7-9 mm across, in fairly compact flowering heads. The lobed, shiny leaves can be used in salads. The stem-leaves clasp the stem at their base, and the uppermost stem-leaves are undivided.

Size	To 1 m
Habitat	Roadsides, ditches, river banks, damp hedges.
Range	Throughout lowlands, but less common in N.
Flowers	May-August

GARLIC MUSTARD *Alliaria petiolata*

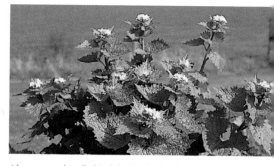

Also commonly called Jack-by-the-hedge. Familiar plant of hedgerows and also sometimes a garden weed. Large heart-shaped leaves are characteristic and smell like garlic when crushed. The flowering heads consist of white flowers, each about 6 mm across, with petals twice as long as **sepals**.

Size	To 1.2 m
Habitat	Wood margins, hedgerows, shaded gardens.
Range	Throughout lowlands. Scattered in Ireland and absent from much of N and W Scotland.
Flowers	April-June

HEDGE MUSTARD *Sisymbrium officinale*

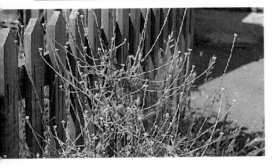

A large, straggly weed with small yellow flowers, each only about 3 mm across. The branches are held stiffly out from the main stem and the fruits are thin **pods** that lie close to the branches. The base leaves are deeply lobed.

Size	To 1 m
Habitat	Common weed of waste ground, roadsides, hedges and arable fields.
Range	Throughout, but not in high hills and mountains.
Flowers	June-July

THALE CRESS *Arabidopsis thaliana*

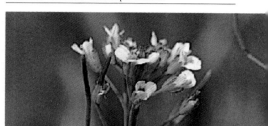

A small plant with almost leafless stems rising from a
rosette of spoon-shaped leaves at its base. The stem leaves
are narrow and unstalked. The flowers are about 10 mm
across with narrow pale yellow petals, about twice as long
as the **sepals**.

Size	To 50 cm
Habitat	Mainly on dry, especially sandy, soils, on walls, banks, and a garden weed.
Range	Throughout, but scattered in W Scotland and in Ireland.
Flowers	April-May

WILD MIGNONETTE *Reseda lutea*

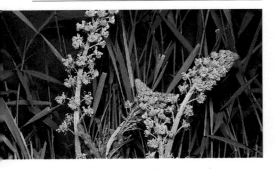

The deeply lobed leaves and narrow, rather compact yellow flower **spikes** make this species easy to identify. Each flower is about 6 mm across. Unlike the garden Mignonette, it is scentless.

Size To 75 cm

Habitat Waste ground, arable field margins, especially on chalky soils.

Range Mainly in the E half of Britain. Scattered and more coastal in W and N, to about Argyll and Moray in Scotland. Introduced and rarer in Ireland.

Flowers June-August

Similar species Weld, *Reseda luteola*, is a taller version, with narrow, unlobed leaves. June-August.

SWEET VIOLET *Viola odorata*

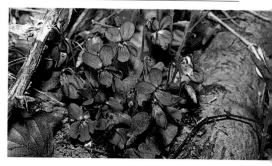

Has white or violet, sweet-smelling flowers, about 15 mm across. Puts out **runners** from which new plants grow. The leaves are long-stalked and heart-shaped at the base, with rather wavy edges. Used in herbal medicine to treat respiratory disorders.

Size To 10 cm tall

Habitat Woodland, hedgerows, banks, railway cuttings, scrub, especially on chalky soils; often escapes from gardens.

Range England, Wales; rather local in Scotland and Ireland.

Flowers February-April

HAIRY VIOLET *Viola hirta*

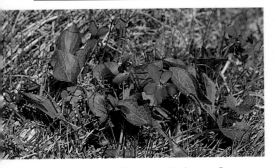

Rather like Sweet Violet (p.41), but its flowers are unscented and paler violet, and its leaves are more triangular and narrower. Each flower is 15 mm across. It has obvious hairs on its stems and leaf stalks.

Size To 5 cm
Habitat Chalk grassland, scrub and open woods.
Range Mainly England and Wales; SE coastal Scotland. Rare in Ireland.
Flowers April-May

COMMON DOG-VIOLET *Viola riviniana*

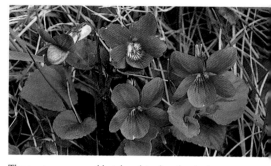

The most common wild violet, this plant has leafy stems with heart-shaped leaves. The flowers are 15-20 mm across, and bluish-violet in colour with a pale **spur**.

Size	To 15 cm, but very variable
Habitat	Woods and hedges, but also pastures and mountain rocks
Range	Common throughout
Flowers	April-June
Similar species	Early Dog-violet, *Viola reichenbachiana*, has a darker spur. S, E and central England. March-May.

HEATH DOG-VIOLET *Viola canina*

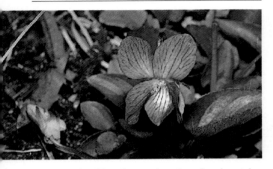

This plant has bluer flowers than the other dog-violets (p.43), each 15-25 mm across with a yellowish **spur**. The leaves are thick and narrowly triangular.

Size To 20 cm
Habitat Rarer than other dog-violets. Heaths, dry grassland, dunes and fens. Not in woodland.
Range Scattered throughout
Flowers April-June

MOUNTAIN PANSY *Viola lutea*

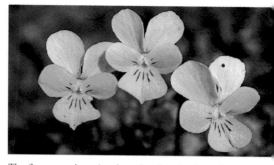

The flowers are large (to about 3 cm) and either yellow, purple or a mixture of the two. The lower leaves are oval, the upper leaves **lanceolate**. All leaves are sparsely hairy, expecially on the veins and edges. The **stipules** are divided into 3-5 lobes. The plants have creeping **rhizomes**.

Size	To 15 cm
Habitat	Grassland and rocky ledges in hilly areas, to about 1000 m.
Range	Hills and mountains of Scotland, Wales and N England; very local in Ireland.
Flowers	June-August

FIELD PANSY *Viola arvensis*

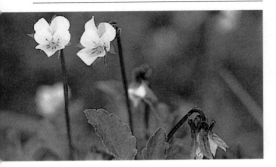

Has small creamy-white flowers, each with a yellow centre, and each about 15 mm in width. The **sepals** are pointed and often longer than the petals. The **stipules** are deeply lobed, with a large, toothed end-lobe.

Size About 15 cm

Habitat Common weed of cultivated and waste ground, especially on neutral or chalky soils.

Range Throughout, but commoner in E half of Britain and SE Ireland.

Flowers April-October

Similar species Wild Pansy, *Viola tricolor*, has larger yellow, white or purple flowers, April-September. Throughout, but less common in chalky areas of lowland England.

COMMON MILKWORT *Polygala vulgaris*

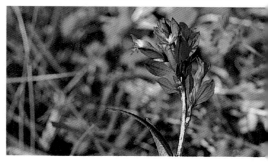

Rather variable in size and in flower colour. The flowers (each up to 8 mm) resemble those of the Pea Family (pp. 75–86) and are blue, pink or white. The stems are thin and feeble, with narrow, alternate leaves.

Size	To 30 cm
Habitat	Grassland, heaths and dunes
Range	Throughout
Flowers	May–September
Similar species	Heath Milkwort, *Polygala serpyllifolia*, more slender stems, opposite leaves and bright blue flowers, May–August. Throughout.

PERFORATE ST JOHN'S WORT *Hypericum perforatum*

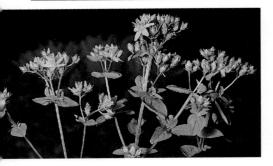

One of the most common of our several St John's Worts. Has upright flowering stems, with opposite pairs of oval stalkless leaves covered in translucent spots. The flowers are yellow, 5-petalled and about 2 cm across. Used in the Middle Ages to treat wounds. The oil has anti-bacterial properties, and soothes burns.

Size To 1 m
Habitat Open woods, hedgerows, waste ground, and grassland.
Range Throughout, but rare in central and W Scotland.
Flowers June-September

COMMON ROCK-ROSE *Helianthemum chamaecistus*

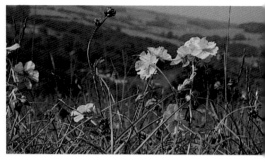

Creeping plant with woody stems and bright yellow flowers (about 2 cm across) with 5 petals. Rather weak, slender stems with narrow, opposite leaves. The leaves are whitish below and tend to curl over at the edges.

Size To 30 cm (often smaller).
Habitat Chalky grassland and scrub.
Range Throughout most of Britain; very rare in Ireland, only in one locality in Co. Donegal.
Flowers June-September

BLADDER CAMPION *Silene vulgaris*

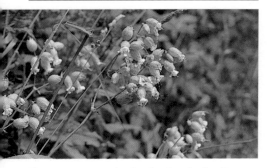

This species is very closely related to the Sea Campion (p.51). It has white flowers and a bladder-like **calyx** behind the petals. The flowers are about 18 mm across. The leaves are oval and pointed, with wavy edges.

Size To 1 m

Habitat Grows on waste ground and in hedgerows and banks.

Range Throughout most of Britain, though rarer in N and W. Scattered in Ireland, mainly central.

Flowers June-August

SEA CAMPION   *Silene maritima*

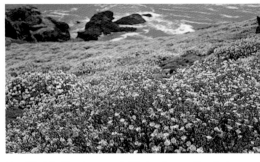

Very like Bladder Campion (p.50) but has smaller, fleshy leaves, larger flowers and a lower growth habit. Like Bladder Campion, this species has a bladder-like **calyx**. The flowers are 2-2.5 cm across.

Size Low cushions or mats, to about 25 cm high.
Habitat Shingle and cliffs, mostly by the sea.
Range Throughout, almost always at the coast.
Flowers June-August

WHITE CAMPION *Silene alba*

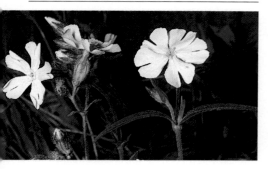

An attractive plant, whose large white flowers (to 3 cm across) remain fully open into the evening, and attract moths as pollinators. Male and female flowers grow on different plants. The leaves are oval or **lanceolate**. Unlike Bladder Campion (p.50) and Sea Campion (p.51) it does not have a bladder-like **calyx**.

Size	To 1 m
Habitat	Waste ground, rough field margins, hedgerows.
Range	Common in most of lowland Britain. Rare in Ireland, Wales, SW England and highland Scotland.
Flowers	May-September

RED CAMPION *Silene dioica*

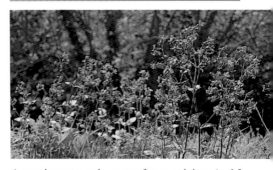

A very decorative early summer flower, with large (to 2.5 cm across) red or deep pink flowers. Slightly smaller plant than White Campion (p.52), with rather smaller flowers. Flowers open in the day to attract bees and butterflies. Where it grows close to White Campion, hybrids with pink flowers are sometimes found. The leaves are oval or oblong. There are separate male and female plants.

Size To 80 cm

Habitat More of a woodland edge flower (even under partial shade of trees) than White Campion. Also hedgerows and roadsides, especially near woods.

Range Common in much of Britain, but rarer in Ireland, W Scotland and also parts of E England.

Flowers May-July

RAGGED ROBIN *Lychnis flos-cuculi*

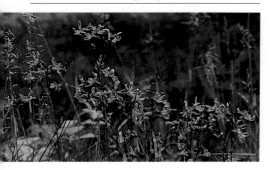

The large flowers are rose-pink (occasionally white) and each of the five petals is deeply divided into four, giving this flower a ragged, almost scruffy, appearance. Each flower is 2.5 cm across. The leaves are narrow and **lanceolate**, and rough to the touch.

Size	To 80 cm
Habitat	Wet meadows, fens and marshes, also wet woodland. Reduced by drainage and fertilization of lowland grassland.
Range	Throughout
Flowers	May–June

FIELD MOUSE-EAR *Cerastium arvense*

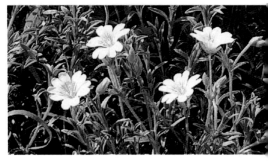

Rather large white flowers (to about 2 cm across) on thin, hairy stalks. The five white petals are deeply notched and longer than the **sepals**. The leaves are narrow and slightly hairy, giving this **genus** its common name.

Size	To 20 cm
Habitat	Dry banks, dry grassland, especially in sandy or slightly acid soils.
Range	Mainly in E. Rare in W and SW.
Flowers	April-August

COMMON MOUSE-EAR *Cerastium fontanum*

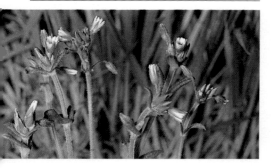

Very common weed with rather trailing, hairy stems.
Grouped white flowers are rather small (8-15 mm across,
but very variable) with five notched petals, about the same
length or slightly longer than the **sepals**. The leaves are
narrow and hairy, hence its common name.

Size To 40 cm
Habitat Grassland, shingle, tracks, sand dunes, cultivated
and waste ground.
Range Common throughout
Flowers April-September

GREATER STITCHWORT *Stellaria holostea*

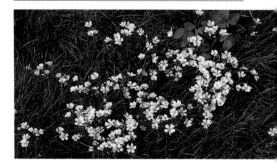

One of our prettiest woodland and hedgerow spring flowers. The white flowers, up to 3 cm across, grow on slender stalks. The petals are notched and longer than the green **sepals**. The leaves are narrow and stiff.

Size	To 60 cm
Habitat	Hedges, banks and wood margins.
Range	Common throughout most of Britain and Ireland, but rarer or absent in extreme N and W.
Flowers	April-June

PINK FAMILY

LESSER STITCHWORT *Stellaria graminea*

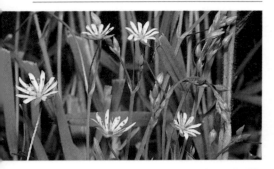

A more delicate plant than Greater Stitchwort (p.57), with smaller flowers and narrower leaves. The flowers are white and up to 10 mm across. The petals are deeply notched, and only just longer than the green **sepals**.

Size	To 60 cm
Habitat	Dry, heathy ground.
Range	Common throughout most of Britain and Ireland.
Flowers	May-August

COMMON CHICKWEED *Stellaria media*

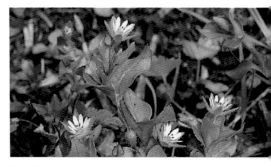

One of our most common weeds, it has very straggly growth and weak, juicy stems. Its white flowers are small, 5-10 mm across, with petals shorter than the green **sepals**. Often given to budgerigars and other cage birds. The leaves can be eaten in salads. Used as herbal medicine for skin diseases.

Size To 30cm, but very variable.
Habitat Mostly on cultivated ground, especially as a weed in vegetable gardens. Also at edges of pastures, and on waste ground.
Range Common throughout
Flowers January-December

SEA SANDWORT *Honkenya peploides*

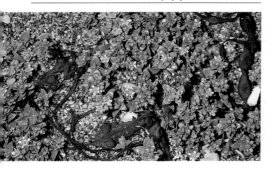

A small plant with broad, fleshy leaves. The stems grow close together, forming tight clumps in the dunes, or between pebbles on shingle beaches. The flowers are yellowish white and up to 10 mm across. The petals are about the same length or shorter than the **sepals**. The fruits are large, green and pea-like.

Size   To 5 cm
Habitat   Dunes and shingle, near the sea.
Range   Common on all coasts.
Flowers   May-August

Thyme-leaved Sandwort *Arenaria serpyllifolia*

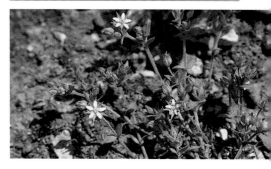

A small, common weed with inconspicuous white flowers, up to 8 mm across, in branched **flowerheads**. The petals are often shorter than the green **sepals**. The fruits are flask-shaped. Its leaves are small, about 6 mm long, and look like Thyme leaves, and its stems are hairy.

Size	To 20 cm
Habitat	Bare, waste ground, either chalky or sandy, quarries, cliffs, dunes. Also grows on the tops of walls.
Range	Throughout most of British Isles. Scattered in most of W Scotland and Ireland.
Flowers	April-November

CORN SPURREY *Spergula arvensis*

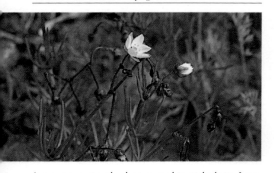

A grey-green, straggly plant covered in sticky hairs. Long, narrow leaves grow in circular clusters (**whorls**) up the stems. The flowers are white, with five petals which are slightly longer than the **sepals**, and about 5 mm across. The fruits are **capsules** which turn downwards and split into five when ripe, releasing blackish seeds.

Size	To 50 cm
Habitat	A weed of light, sandy soils, often in cornfields. Much reduced by herbicides.
Range	Throughout
Flowers	June–August

GREATER SEA-SPURREY *Spergularia media*

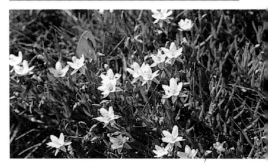

A pretty white or pale pink seaside flower. Each flower is up to 12 mm across, its five petals longer than its **sepals**. The leaves are fleshy. It produces a fruit **capsule** of about 10 mm in length, which contains large, flattened seeds.

Size	To 30 cm
Habitat	Saltmarshes
Range	Throughout, but not as widespread as Lesser Sea-spurrey (see below).
Flowers	June-September
Similar species	Lesser Sea-spurrey, *Spergularia marina*; smaller pink flowers, petals shorter than sepals. Prefers drier parts of saltmarshes and inland salty soils. June-August.

SPRINGBEAUTY *Montia perfoliata*

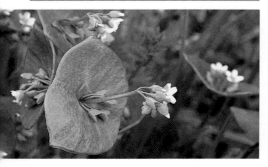

Unmistakable, with its small white flowers set against two shiny leaves which are completely joined around the stem. The flowers are about 2 mm across.

Size To 30 cm
Habitat Waste and cultivated ground, especially on sandy soils. Also on dunes.
Range Introduced from N America. Mainly in eastern part of Britain. Rare in Ireland.
Flowers May-July

COMMON MALLOW *Malva sylvestris*

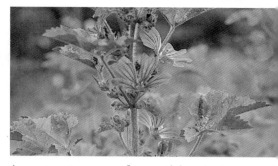

A very attractive common flower, with large (to 4 cm across) pink flowers. Each of the five petals is marked with dark stripes. The leaves, which are large with rounded lobes, can be eaten in salads.

Size	To 1 m
Habitat	Waste ground, roadsides.
Range	Common in England; scattered in Wales, Scotland and Ireland.
Flowers	June-September
Similar species	Dwarf Mallow, *Malva neglecta*, is low, with smaller, paler flowers, mainly S and E England. June-September.

TREE MALLOW *Lavatera arborea*

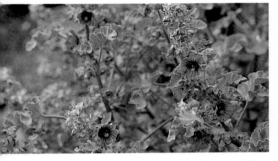

Looks like a giant, hairy version of the Common Mallow (p.65). This magnificent bushy plant has tall **spikes** of large pink-purple flowers, each 3-5 cm across. The roundish, velvety leaves are up to 20 cm across. The tall stems can be quite woody, hence the name 'Tree' Mallow. Makes a fine garden plant.

Size	To 3 m
Habitat	Rocks and waste ground near the sea.
Range	S and W coasts
Flowers	July-September

MARSH MALLOW *Althaea officinalis*

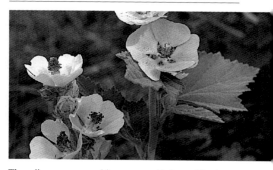

The tall, grey stems and leaves are softly hairy. The leaves are sharply toothed and sometimes folded like a fan. The flowers are a delicate shade of palest pink, and up to 5 cm across. Extracts of Marsh Mallow are used to treat inflammation and ulcers. Also the source of the original marshmallow sweets.

Size To 1.2 m

Habitat Brackish ditches and banks near the sea, and at upper (landward) end of saltmarshes.

Range Coasts of S Wales, S and E England and S and W Ireland.

Flowers August-September

FAIRY FLAX *Linum catharticum*

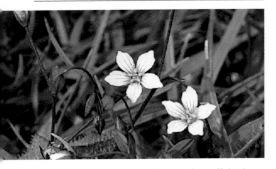

A delicate, inconspicuous plant with small (4-6 mm across), white, five-petalled flowers, held up on thin, wiry stems. Although common, easily overlooked. The leaves are oblong and grow in opposite pairs.

Size To 25 cm
Habitat Grassland, heaths, moorland, dunes, rock ledges.
Range Throughout
Flowers June-September
Similar species Cultivated Flax, *Linum usitatissimum*, is commonly grown as a crop (linen and linseed oil), especially in E England. The flowers turn entire fields a bright pale blue in summer.

DOVE'S FOOT CRANESBILL *Geranium molle*

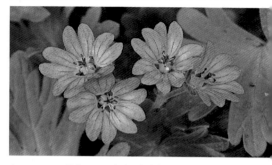

A common wild flower with deeply lobed, hairy leaves and
hairy stems. The flowers are bright pink-purple (sometimes
white) and up to 10 mm across. Like all cranesbills, the
fruit has the long beak which gives this group its name, but
in this species the fruit is hairless.

Size	To 40 cm
Habitat	Dry grassland, waste land, dunes
Range	Common throughout
Flowers	April-September
Similar species	Small-flowered Cranesbill, *Geranium pusillum*, pale lilac flowers, 6 mm across, June-September, and hairy fruits. Common in England.

CRANESBILL FAMILY

HERB ROBERT *Geranium robertianum*

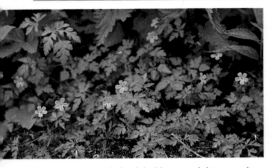

A pretty species with five-lobed leaves and thin, spreading, reddish stems. The flowers are 12-16 mm across and have five pink petals, with rounded ends. The **sepals** are red.

Size	To 50 cm
Habitat	Woods, hedges, banks, rocks, shingle, and as an attractive weed in gardens.
Range	Common throughout, but rarer in parts of N and NW. Scotland
Flowers	May-September

MEADOW CRANESBILL *Geranium pratense*

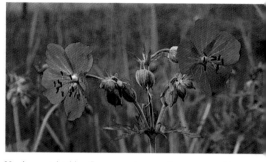

Has large violet-blue flowers, each up to 4 cm across, with rounded petals, on long flower stalks. The leaves are rather feathery, being deeply cut, and have 5-7 lobes. Often grows in patches.

Size	To 1 m
Habitat	Meadows and roadsides
Range	Widespread in England and S Scotland. Rare in Ireland and local in Wales and N and W. Scotland.
Flowers	June-September
Similar species	Wood Cranesbill, *Geranium sylvaticum*, a smaller, reddish-violet flowers, June-July, central and S Scotland and N England.

COMMON STORKSBILL *Erodium cicutarium*

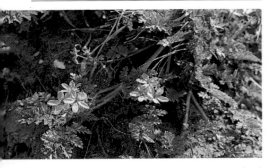

The flowers are a bright pink-purple (sometimes white) and about 7-16 mm across. The feathery leaves often grow as a **rosette** at the base of the plant. In storksbills the fruit is very long (in this case about 4 cm) and beak-shaped.

Size To 60 cm

Habitat Dry grassland, arable fields on light soils and dunes.

Range Common around all coasts. Scattered inland in England.

Flowers June-September

WOOD-SORREL *Oxalis acetosella*

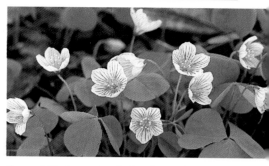

Shamrock-like leaves identify this plant of the woodland floor. The large flowers are white, with five delicate petals veined in lilac, and up to 15 mm across.

Size	To 15 cm
Habitat	Woods, hedges, shady rocks, mainly on acid soils.
Range	Throughout, but rare in chalk and fenland areas of E Anglia.
Flowers	April-May

INDIAN BALSAM *Impatiens glandulifera*

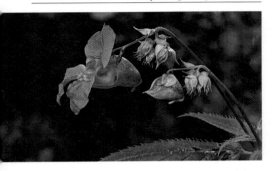

Also called Policeman's Helmet. Introduced from Himalaya, it is a tall, hollow-stemmed plant with large opposite leaves and big purple-pink flowers, to about 4 cm long, with **spurs**. The fruits are oval **capsules** which explode when ripe and dry, releasing the seeds.

Size	To 2 m
Habitat	River banks and wet waste places. Often by polluted streams in industrial areas.
Range	Scattered throughout, except N and W. Scotland. Most common in N England.
Flowers	July-October
Similar species	Touch-me-not Balsam, *Impatiens noli- tangere*, smaller, with yellow, brown-spotted flowers.

COMMON RESTHARROW *Ononis repens*

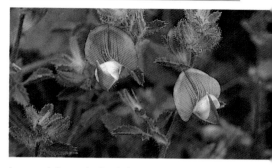

Large, pink flowers (to 2 cm) characterize this restharrow, a pretty species with hairy stems. The leaves are usually made up of three toothed leaflets, but sometimes of only one leaflet. Spreads by sending out **rhizomes** which used to get caught in ploughs and harrows, hence its name.

Size	To 40 cm
Habitat	Rough grassland, mainly on chalky soils, sand dunes
Range	Common, but rare in N and W, where mainly coastal.
Flowers	June-September
Similar species	Spiny Restharrow, *Ononis spinosa*, taller, with spines. England, not SW. June-September.

BLACK MEDICK   *Medicago lupulina*

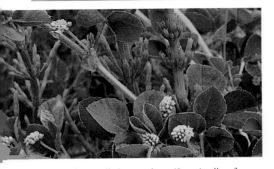

This plant has small clusters of tiny (3 mm) yellow flowers, which later turn into black kidney-shaped **pods** in late summer and autumn. The leaves are a typical three-lobed cloverleaf, but the tip of each is extended into a minute point.

Size	To 50 cm
Habitat	Grassland, roadsides
Range	Widespread, except in N and NW of both Ireland and Scotland.
Flowers	April-August
Similar species	Spotted Medick, *Medicago arabica*, has a black spot on each leaflet; mainly S and E England, and S Wales, April-August.

TALL MELILOT *Melilotus altissima*

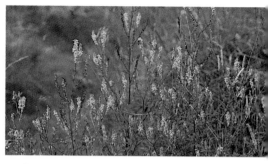

A tall species, with spikes of small (5-7 mm long), yellow flowers. The leaves each have three leaflets. The leaflets are about 15-30 mm long, oblong and toothed. The ripe fruits are hairy, black oval **pods**.

Size To 1.5 m

Habitat Fields, roadsides and waste places

Range Lowland England, especially S and E. Rare and usually coastal elsewhere.

Flowers June-August

Similar species Ribbed (Common) Melilot, *Melilotus officinalis*, has small yellow flowers (4-7 mm long) and hairless brown seed pods. Lowland England, rare elsewhere. June-September.

RED CLOVER *Trifolium pratense*

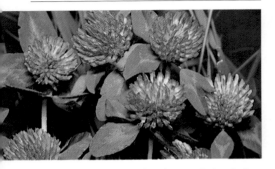

The leaves are large typical cloverleaves with three leaflets. In Red Clover these often have pale white semicircular markings. The **flowerheads** are rounded and pink and up to 4 cm long. Used in herbal medicine to treat respiratory and skin disorders.

Size	To 60 cm
Habitat	Grassy banks, roadsides, meadows
Range	Throughout
Flowers	May-September

WHITE CLOVER *Trifolium repens*

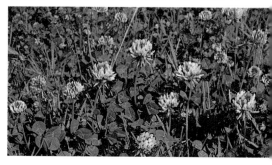

Commonest of the clovers, found in most types of grassland. The leaves are typical cloverleaf shape, with three leaflets. Like Red Clover (p.78), the leaflets normally have a pale band, but are sometimes heart-shaped. The flowers are white and clustered in heads of up to about 2 cm across.

Size	To 50 cm
Habitat	Grassy banks, grassland, lawns
Range	Throughout
Flowers	June-September

KIDNEY VETCH *Anthyllis vulneraria*

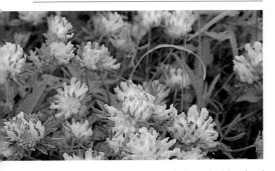

This species has large, rather tightly packed heads of yellow, cream or red flowers at the top of a long stalk. The **flowerheads** are in pairs, each to about 4 cm across. After flowering, the heads become downy (the **calyces** are woolly). The leaves are hairy and made up of nine leaflets.

Size	To 60 cm
Habitat	Dry, usually chalky soils, often coastal, frequently in grassland on cliff-tops.
Range	Widespread throughout
Flowers	June-September

BIRDSFOOT TREFOIL *Lotus corniculatus*

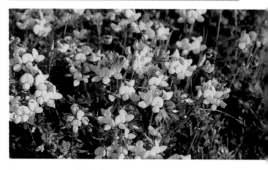

A common, nearly hairless plant with large, bright yellow flowers. The **flowerheads** are made up of about six flowers, each up to 15 mm long and sometimes streaked with red. The leaves have three main leaflets, and there is also a pair of smaller leaflets at base of the leaf-stalk.

Size	To 40 cm
Habitat	Grassland
Range	Throughout
Flowers	June-September
Similar species	Greater Birdsfoot Trefoil, *Lotus uliginosus*, 60 cm, has a hollow stem, and heads of 8+ flowers, June-August. Damp habitats throughout, but rare in central Ireland and N and NW Scotland.

SAINFOIN *Onobrychis viciifolia*

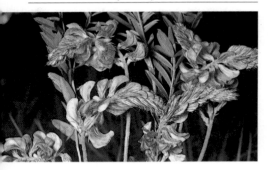

A beautiful plant with tall **spikes** of pink flowers (each flower about 15 mm long) on long stems. It has pretty leaves with 6-12 pairs of leaflets. Often escaped from cultivation (it is used as a forage crop for livestock), but a native form also exists. The name comes from the French and means healthy hay – a reference to its use as animal fodder.

Size	To 60 cm
Habitat	Chalk and limestone grassland
Range	Mainly S and E England (to S Yorkshire)
Flowers	June-August

Tufted Vetch   *Vicia cracca*

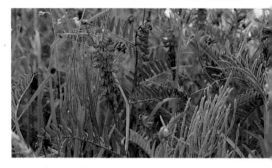

A fine climbing plant, with long **spikes** of blue or purple flowers, each flower to 12 mm long. There are up to 40 flowers in each spike. The leaves are made up of many paired leaflets and each leaf ends in a branched **tendril**.

Size To 2 m
Habitat Hedges, rough grassland, meadows
Range Throughout, except highlands
Flowers June-August

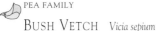

BUSH VETCH *Vicia sepium*

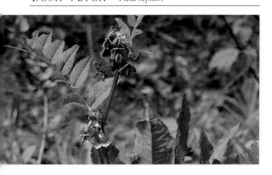

A climbing plant with short **spikes** of pale blue or purple flowers, each flower 12-15 mm long. The leaves, each made up of 2-3 pairs of leaflets, end in a branched **tendril**. Unlike the slightly hairy Common Vetch (p.85), this plant is almost hairless.

Size	To 1 m
Habitat	Hedges, woodland edges and rough grassland
Range	Throughout, except highlands
Flowers	May-August

COMMON VETCH   *Vicia sativa*

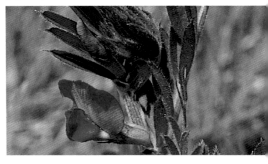

The flowers of the Common Vetch are purple and usually single or in pairs. Each flower is 10-18 mm long. The leaves are made up of 3-8 pairs of leaflets. This plant is slightly hairy, unlike the almost hairless Bush Vetch (p.84).

Size	To 1.2 m
Habitat	Grassy areas, roadsides, waste places
Range	Throughout lowlands, scattered in Ireland
Flowers	May-September

PEA FAMILY

MEADOW VETCHLING *Lathyrus pratensis*

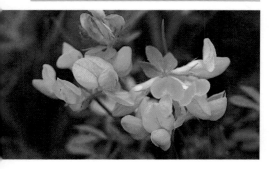

A common plant, with pale yellow flowers in clusters of up to 10. Each flower is 15-18 mm long. It has leaves made up of one or two pairs of leaflets, and branched **tendrils** with which it clambers up grass stems and other plants.

Size	To 1.2 m
Habitat	Hedges, long grass
Range	Common throughout, except Scottish Highlands
Flowers	May-August

MEADOWSWEET *Filipendula ulmaria*

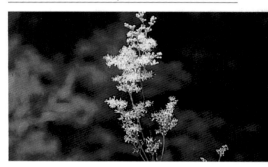

One of the prettiest wild flowers of marshy habitats. The small, creamy-white flowers, each about 4-8 mm across, are arranged in rather untidy clusters. The leaves have 2-5 pairs of leaflets and, when crushed, give off a distinctive, rather antiseptic smell. Once used to flavour mead, hence the name. This is the plant which first gave us aspirin, and it is still used as a herbal remedy for fevers, and for treating diarrhoea.

Size To 1.2 m
Habitat Marshes, fens, river banks, damp meadows and other wet places.
Range Throughout
Flowers June-September

SILVERWEED *Potentilla anserina*

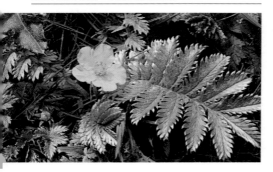

Best recognized by the silvery-backed **compound** leaves,
with leaflets arranged in pairs. It has large yellow flowers
(to about 2 cm across), with five petals. Frequently forms
large patches over damp disturbed or trampled ground.

Size	To 15 cm
Habitat	Dunes, wet pastures, roadsides, margins of ponds
Range	Throughout, except Scottish Highlands
Flowers	June-August

TORMENTIL *Potentilla erecta*

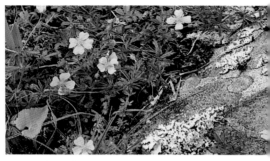

Tormentil has yellow flowers, about 10-15 mm across, each with four petals. The leaves are a shiny green, and most are made up of three rather narrow leaflets. The plant has a tough, woody base from which the stems and flowers grow up each year. Used in herbal medicine to treat diarrhoea and sore throats.

Size To 30 cm
Habitat Heathy grassland, bogs, fens, mountains, mostly on acid soils.
Range Throughout
Flowers June-September

ROSE FAMILY

CREEPING CINQUEFOIL *Potentilla reptans*

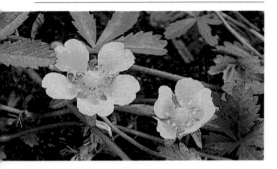

Spreads by sending out long, creeping **runners** which root at intervals. The flowers are large (to 2.5 cm across) and yellow, with five petals. The **compound** leaves are made up of five (occasionally seven) narrow leaflets, which fan out from a central point. The name cinquefoil comes from the French word *cinque* meaning 'five'.

Size To 20 cm

Habitat Hedges, banks, roadsides, grassland, waste places, mainly on neutral or alkaline soils.

Range Throughout, but rare in central and N Scotland, and scattered in N Ireland.

Flowers June-September

BARREN STRAWBERRY *Potentilla sterilis*

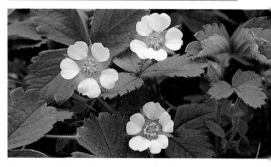

This is one of the earliest of our woodland species to come into flower. The Barren Strawberry looks very like the true Wild Strawberry (p.92), but it lacks the silky hairs under the leaves. The flowers are white and about 10-15 mm across, with gaps between the petals. It does not have the fleshy, edible fruits of Wild Strawberry, hence its common name.

Size To 15 cm
Habitat Open woodland, woodland edges and scrub
Range Throughout, but rarer in N Scotland
Flowers February-May

ROSE FAMILY

WILD STRAWBERRY *Fragaria vesca*

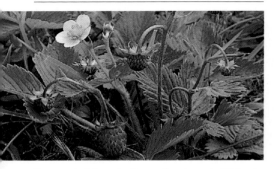

Distinguished from the Barren Strawberry (p.91) by the silky hairs under its leaves, its larger petals and by its fruits. The flowers are white, about 12-18 mm across, with touching or slightly overlapping petals. The fruits are small, but delicious, red strawberries. Like the cultivated Garden Strawberry, *Fragaria* x *ananassa*, it spreads by rooting from **runners**.

Size To 30 cm
Habitat Woods, clearings and scrub, especially on lime-rich soils.
Range Throughout, but rarer in N Scotland
Flowers April-July

WOOD AVENS *Geum urbanum*

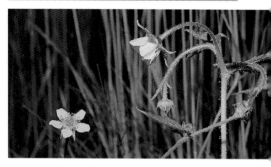

Also known as Herb Bennet, from the old Latin *Herba benedicta*, 'blessed herb'. A straggly plant with tall, hairy stems, and toothed stem leaves. The yellow flowers look a bit like cinquefoils (p.90), but are small (8-15 mm across) and inconspicuous. They turn into tight, slightly prickly fruit heads. Used to treat piles and digestive disorders.

Size	To 60 cm
Habitat	Scrub, hedges
Range	Common throughout, except N Scotland and Scottish Highlands.
Flowers	June-August
Similar species	Water Avens, *Geum rivale*, orange-pink to purplish nodding flowers, May-September. Scattered, especially N, rare in SE. Scattered in Ireland.

AGRIMONY *Agrimonia eupatoria*

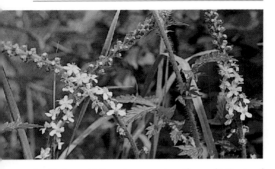

A tall plant with large leaves, each made up of 3-6 pairs of toothed leaflets. The flowering heads are long **spikes** with many yellow flowers, each about 5-8 mm across. Agrimony has many uses in herbal medicine, including the treatment of gallstones and ulcers and to stop bleeding.

Size	To 80 cm
Habitat	Hedgebanks, roadsides
Range	Throughout, but only scattered in Scotland
Flowers	June-August

LADY'S MANTLE *Alchemilla vulgaris*

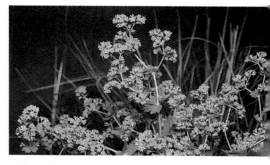

A plant with pretty, soft green leaves with rounded lobes, and heads of tiny yellow-green flowers, each only 3-4 mm across. The flowers have no petals, but the yellowish **sepals** are petal-like. The name *Alchemilla* comes from the word 'alchemy'; the water drops found on the leaves after rain were gathered by alchemists and used in magic potions. Lady's Mantle has a long history of medicinal use; it was used to treat cuts.

Size	To 50 cm
Habitat	Meadows, pastures, roadsides, up to 1200 m in hilly areas.
Range	Throughout, but rare in SE England and SE Ireland
Flowers	June-September

SALAD BURNET *Sanguisorba minor*

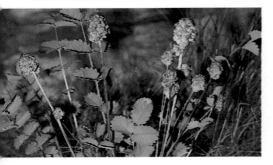

Best identified by the **pinnate** leaves at the base of the plant. The reddish flowering stems are thin and stiff and the flowers develop in tight, rounded heads, 7-12 mm across. The female flowers are at the top, the male flowers towards the bottom. The leaves are good to eat, tasting of cucumber.

Size	To 30 cm
Habitat	Chalk and limestone grassland
Range	Common in England, rare in Scotland, rare in Wales (except N and S coasts) and local in Ireland.
Flowers	April-August
Similar species	Great Burnet, *Sanguisorba officinalis*, larger with oblong, red **flowerheads**. Mainly central and N England. Mostly absent from Scotland and rare in Ireland.

BITING STONECROP *Sedum acre*

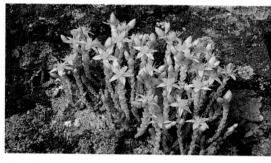

Also called Wall-pepper, from the strong peppery taste of its leaves and its habit of growing on dry walls. The leaves are small, fleshy and hairless. The flowers are bright yellow and star-shaped, about 12 mm across, with 5 petals.

Size To 10 cm
Habitat Dunes, dry grassland, dry rocks, walls, roofs
Range Throughout, but more scattered in Scotland
Flowers June-July

WALL PENNYWORT *Umbilicus rupestris*

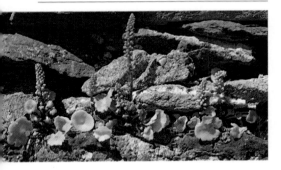

Also called Navelwort from the shape of the shiny, circular leaves which have a navel-like centre. The tubular flowers are whitish-green, 8-10 mm long and clustered in a long spike.

Size To 40 cm
Habitat Rocks and walls
Range W. and SW. England, Wales, SW. Scotland, Ireland (especially S and W.).
Flowers June-August

MEADOW SAXIFRAGE *Saxifraga granulata*

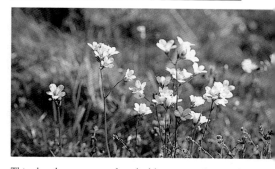

This plant has a **rosette** of toothed leaves at its base, and small **bulbils** (tiny bulbs). In late spring the hairy flowering stalks grow up amongst grass and reveal pretty white flowers, each about 2 cm across. After flowering and producing seed the main plant dies, leaving the bulbils near the surface of the soil. These grow into new plants the following spring.

Size	To 50 cm
Habitat	Old grassland, especially on chalk or limestone
Range	Mainly in E Britain. Rare in Ireland, where probably introduced.
Flowers	April-June

RUE-LEAVED SAXIFRAGE *Saxifraga tridactylites*

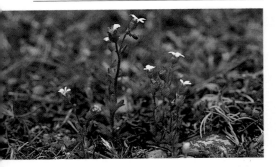

A small, hairy plant with red stems. The leaves each have 3-5 leaflets and the tiny flowers (only 4-6 mm across) are white, with 5 petals. In dry places the leaves may be reddish.

Size To 10 cm
Habitat Dunes, dry grassland, old walls, rocks
Range Throughout England and Wales, but rather rare and local in Scotland. In Ireland most common in central areas and mid-west.
Flowers April-June

PURPLE LOOSESTRIFE *Lythrum salicaria*

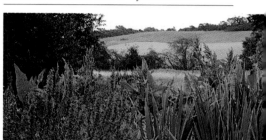

A strikingly handsome flower of wet places. The leaves are narrow and hairy, and the red-purple flowers are grouped in showy **spikes** up to about 30 cm long. A patch of Purple Loosestrife in full flower adds a splash of colour to many swampy habitats in midsummer.

Size	To 1.2 m
Habitat	River banks, lake margins, reedswamps and marshes
Range	Throughout England, Wales and Ireland. In Scotland, only common in the S and W, and absent from most of central and N Scotland.
Flowers	June-August

GREAT WILLOWHERB *Epilobium hirsutum*

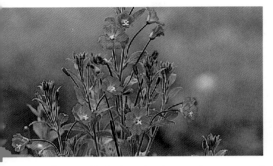

Our largest willowherb, with pale green, hairy stems and large pinkish-purple flowers, to over 2 cm across, each with a whitish eye. The leaves are **lanceolate**, and toothed. Its fruit **pods** are 5-8 cm long, and covered with downy hairs, releasing fluffy white seeds when ripe.

Size	To 1.5 m
Habitat	River banks, marshes, fens
Range	Throughout, except for much of central, N and W. Scotland
Flowers	July-August

Broad-leaved Willowherb *Epilobium montanum*

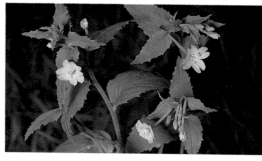

One of the most common willowherbs, it has broad, hairless, stalked leaves. The pale pink flowers are up to 10 mm across. The fruit **pods** are 4-8 cm long, and covered with downy hairs, releasing fluffy white seeds when ripe.

Size	To 60 cm
Habitat	Woods, hedges, roadsides, rocks, walls and as a garden weed
Range	Throughout
Flowers	June-August
Similar species	American Willowherb, *Epilobium ciliatum*, small pink flowers and hairy, often reddish stems.

ROSE-BAY WILLOWHERB *Chamaenerion angustifolium*

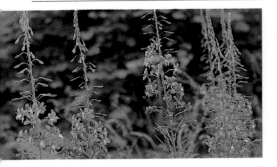

A tall plant with narrow leaves, growing spirally from tall stems. When flowering it is unmistakable, with its handsome **spikes** of large pinkish-purple flowers, each flower 2-3 cm across. As in all willowherbs, the fruit is a long **pod** which opens to release fluffy white seeds.

Size To 1.2 m

Habitat Rocky places, scree slopes, woodland clearings, disturbed ground, industrial areas. Common coloniser of burned ground, especially in clear-felled woods.

Range Throughout, but rare in most of Ireland (except parts of NE) and in N and W. Scotland.

Flowers July-September

ENCHANTER'S NIGHTSHADE *Circaea lutetiana*

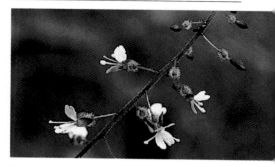

Named after Circe, the enchantress of Greek legend who turned Odysseus' men into pigs by giving them a magic potion. A common woodland plant with rounded shiny leaves, and slender stems with small white flowers held aloft. Each flower is 4-8 mm across.

Size To 70 cm

Habitat Woods, hedges and banks; shady corners of gardens

Range Throughout England, Wales, Ireland and SW. Scotland. Rare in central and N Scotland

Flowers June-August

SANICLE *Sanicula europaea*

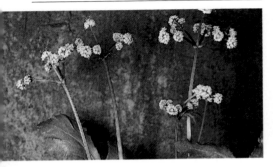

Sanicle has glossy, dark green toothed leaves with 3-5 lobes. The flowers are **umbels** of small pinkish flowers, each flower about 3 mm across. Later these develop into hooked fruits which cling to animal fur or clothing.

Size To 60 cm
Habitat Woodland, especially beech and oak, on rich soils
Range Common, but local, throughout
Flowers May-September

COW PARSLEY *Anthriscus sylvestris*

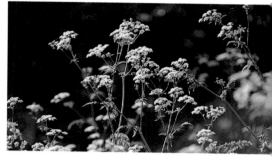

Also known as Queen Anne's Lace, this is the commonest roadside member of the carrot family in southern England. The stems are hollow and the leaves rather feathery, hence the name 'Parsley'. Has abundant white, lace-like flowers in spring, each 3.5-4 mm across, in **umbels** to about 6 cm across.

Size To 1 m
Habitat Roadsides, wood margins, banks
Range Throughout, but commonest in the S, and more local in SW Ireland and N and W Scotland.
Flowers April-June

ROUGH CHERVIL *Chaerophyllum temulentum*

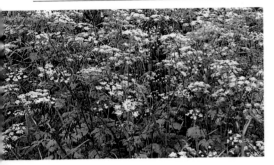

Rather similar to Cow Parsley (p.107), but distinguished by its purple-spotted, hairy stems, with swollen **nodes**. Also by its solid, rather than hollow stems. Comes into flower later than Cow Parsley and Hogweed (p.111). Flowers are white, each about 2 mm across, in **umbels** to about 6 cm across. The hairy, feathery leaves have rounded segments.

Size To 1 m
Habitat Hedges, banks, roadsides, woodland edges
Range Common in England and Wales. Absent from much of Scotland and Ireland, especially the N and W.
Flowers June-July

UPRIGHT HEDGE-PARSLEY *Torilis japonica*

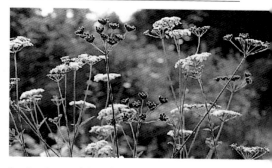

Small rather purplish **umbels**, to about 4 cm across. The leaves are feathery, dark green and hairy. The stems are rough and bristly. The latest of the common roadside members of the carrot family to come into flower, even later than Rough Chervil (p.108).

Size To 1.25 m
Habitat Hedges, banks, roadsides and rough grassland
Range Throughout, but rarer in N and W Scotland
Flowers July-August

SWEET CICELY *Myrrhis odorata*

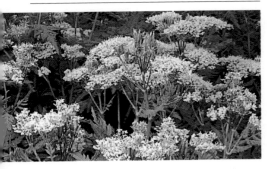

Similar to Cow Parsley (p.107), but has more solid stems. Its leaves are even more feathery, and fern-like with white blotches. The white flowers grow in heads of about 5 cm across. Smells like aniseed.

Size	To 1 m
Habitat	Roadsides
Range	Mainly in N England, N Wales and Scotland
Flowers	May-June

HOGWEED *Heracleum sphondylium*

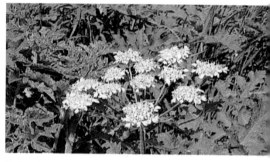

Tall, rather tough, bristly plant with large, lobed leaves. The **umbels** are large (to about 20 cm) and flat, with white flowers up to 10 mm across. The outer flowers have two or three larger petals.

Size To 2 m
Habitat Open woods, roadside verges, grassy banks
Range Throughout
Flowers June-September
Similar species Giant Hogweed, *Heracleum mantegazzianum*, huge, to over 5 m, with umbels to 50 cm across. Introduced, now widespread.

ALEXANDERS *Smyrnium olusatrum*

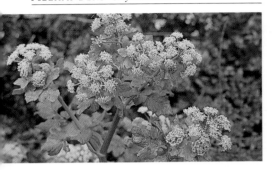

This speciality of the coasts has deep green, glossy leaves and yellow-green flowers (3 mm across) in spring. It tends to take the place of Cow Parsley (p.107) in the hedgerows near the sea (it is probably more sensitive to frosts, which are less frequent in coastal areas). Formerly grown as a herb, and used in cooking like Celery.

Size To 1.5 m

Habitat Hedges, banks, roadsides and waste ground near the sea.

Range Scattered around coasts, especially Wales, S England and E coast of Ireland. Rare in most of Scotland.

Flowers April-June

BURNET-SAXIFRAGE *Pimpinella saxifraga*

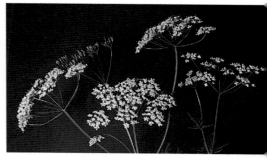

The **pinnate** lower leaves resemble those of Salad Burnet,
(p.96), hence the 'burnet' part of the name. The 'saxifrage'
(p.99) part comes from its habit of growing amongst stones
(sax – stone). It is in fact related to neither. The leaves are
of two distinct kinds; the lower ones have 4-6 pairs of oval,
toothed leaflets, the stem leaves are divided into long,
narrow segments. The small **umbels** of white flowers droop
when young, and are 2-5 cm across.

Size	To 60 cm
Habitat	Dry grassland, mostly on chalk or limestone
Range	Throughout, but rarer in N and W Scotland and N and W Ireland.
Flowers	July-August

GROUND ELDER *Aegopodium podagraria*

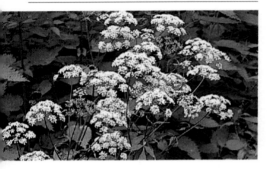

Also called Bishop's Weed. This is one of the major garden weeds, and is very difficult to eradicate because of its **rhizomes** which spread quickly under the soil. The leaves are divided into three toothed leaflets and the stems are hollow. The white flowers grow in **umbels** 2-6 cm across.

Size	To 1 m
Habitat	Waste places, gardens
Range	Throughout
Flowers	May-July

FOOL'S PARSLEY *Aethusa cynapium*

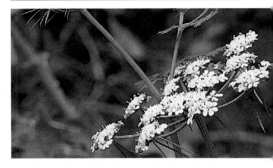

The leaves look a bit like Parsley, but the plant is poisonous – hence the name. The long thin, pointed green **bracts** (specialized leaves) hanging down beneath the **umbels** of small white flowers help to distinguish this species. The **umbels** are 2-6 cm across.

Size	To 1.2 m
Habitat	A weed of waste and cultivated ground, river banks
Range	Throughout lowland Britain, but only scattered and mainly coastal in Scotland. Scattered in Ireland.
Flowers	July-August

HEMLOCK *Conium maculatum*

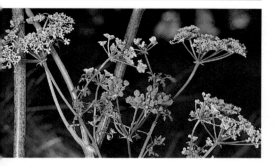

This plant's main claim to fame is that it was used by Socrates, the Greek philosopher, to poison himself. It is one of our most deadly plants, but fortunately has no attractive berries, and smells unpleasant. It is a fine-looking, tall plant with feathery leaves and a purple-blotched stem. The small white flowers are clustered in **umbels** 2-5 cm across.

Size	To 2 m
Habitat	River banks, damp places and waste ground
Range	Throughout the lowlands, but mainly coastal in Scotland
Flowers	June-July

WILD ANGELICA *Angelica sylvestris*

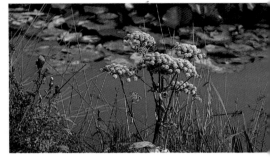

A tall plant, with a purplish colour and inflated leaf stalks. The divided leaves are large, to 60 cm, and have a triangular outline. The **flowerheads** are also large, up to 15 cm across, with white or pinkish flowers.

Size	To 2 m
Habitat	Wet woodland, damp meadows, fens, marshes
Range	Throughout
Flowers	July-September
Similar species	Garden Angelica, *Angelica archangelica*, similar, but flowers greenish, and stems greener (and used to make confectionery).

WILD PARSNIP *Pastinaca sativa*

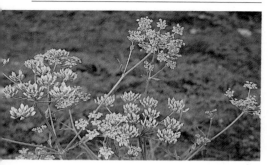

Distinctive, with its yellow flowers, yellow-green leaves and hollow stems. The flowers grow in **umbels** which are 3-10 cm across. The leaves give off a strong smell of parsnip when crushed. Closely related to the cultivated parsnip.

Size	To 1.5 m
Habitat	Roadside verges, dry grassland and disturbed soils, especially on chalk
Range	Mainly S, central and E England
Flowers	July-August

WILD CARROT *Daucus carota*

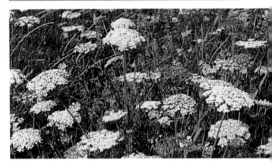

Closely related to the common vegetable, the cultivated carrot. The leaves are feathery with narrow segments, and they smell of carrot. The flowers are mostly white, but at the centre of each **umbel** (to 7 cm across) is a single red or purple flower. The fruiting heads close over into a nest-like shape after flowering. Used as a herbal medicine to treat cystitis and gout.

Size To 1 m
Habitat Grassland and grassy banks, especially on chalky soils; often near the sea.
Range Throughout, but mainly coastal in Scotland
Flowers July-August

CARROT FAMILY

ROCK SAMPHIRE *Crithmum maritimum*

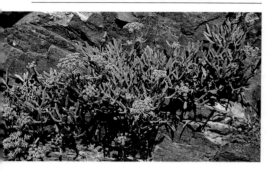

Rock Samphire grows in tight clumps. Its **flowerheads** are
greenish-yellow and grow in **umbels** measuring 3-6 cm
across. The leaves are thick and succulent and can be
eaten, usually when made into a pickle.

Size To 45 cm
Habitat Cliffs and rocks at the coast
Range Coasts around Britain and Ireland, but absent from
E coast north of Suffolk, and from NW Scotland.
Flowers July-October

WHITE BRYONY *Bryonia dioica*

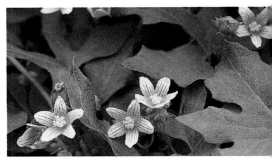

A long, climbing plant, which clings to the branches and foliage of trees and other plants using its winding **tendrils**. The leaves are lobed, and the flowers greenish-white and 10-18 mm across. Male and female flowers grow on separate plants. The female plants produce bright red, poisonous berries in the autumn.

Size	To 6 m long
Habitat	Hedges, scrub, woodland edges
Range	Central, S and E England, E Wales. Not found further N than Northumberland.
Flowers	May-September

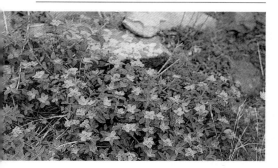

PETTY SPURGE *Euphorbia peplus*

One of the most common spurges, with green **flowerheads** (in threes) and rather blunt, oval leaves. The individual flowers are very small (a few mm across) and arranged in umbel-like groups. The stem is usually branched. Like all spurges, it has a milky, poisonous juice.

Size	To 30 cm
Habitat	Fields, waste land and a weed in gardens
Range	Throughout, but not common in much of Ireland and Scotland
Flowers	May-November
Similar species	Sun Spurge, *Euphorbia helioscopia*, usually unbranched, with yellow-green flowerheads in 5s, May-October. Throughout.

WOOD SPURGE *Euphorbia amygdaloides*

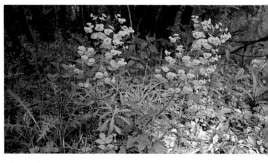

The only spurge commonly found in woods. A big, handsome plant, with a tall, hairy stem. The large, yellow **flowerheads** are arranged in groups of 5-10. As with all spurges, the individual flowers are tiny (just a few mm). The leaves are long and narrow, and measure up to about 8 cm long. The stems and leaves contain a milky, poisonous juice.

Size	To 80 cm
Habitat	Damp woodland, on rich but light soil
Range	South of a line from N Wales to N Norfolk, commonest in the S. Very rare in Ireland (only on S coast).
Flowers	March-May

Dog's Mercury *Mercurialis perennis*

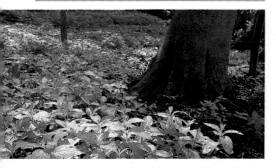

A common woodland plant with flat, oval leaves. Unlike the spurges (p.122, 123), Dog's Mercury does not have milky juice, but like those species, it is poisonous. Its flowers are 3-5 mm long, and grow in **spikes** on male plants and partly hidden by leaves on female plants. Often covers large areas of the woodland floor, and, as male and female plants are separate, big patches can be made up of one sex.

Size To 40 cm
Habitat Woodland, shady rocks on mountains
Range Throughout, but rare in N and W Scotland, and in Ireland
Flowers February-April

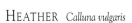

HEATHER *Calluna vulgaris*

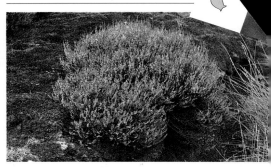

The dominant plant on much upland moor and heath, Heather turns whole hillsides purple when in flower. It has tough, woody stems with small opposite leaves. The flowers are small (about 4 mm long) and numerous, and both petals and **sepals** are pinkish-purple. Also known as Ling.

Size	To 1 m
Habitat	Heath, moorland, bogs
Range	Throughout, wherever the soils are acid
Flowers	July-September

CROSS-LEAVED HEATH *Erica tetralix*

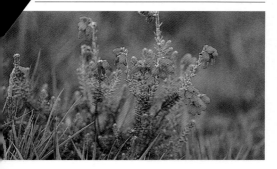

Large (to about 7 mm long), pink tubular flowers grow at the tips of the stems. The leaves are small and narrow and arranged in **whorls** of four. The whole plant is covered in soft hairs. Often grows in large patches like Heather.

Size	To 60 cm
Habitat	Bogs, wet heaths, moorland
Range	Throughout, on wet acid soils
Flowers	July-September
Similar species	Bell Heather, *Erica cinerea*, is similar, but hairless and flowers purplish, 5-6 mm long. Throughout, but local in central England and central Ireland, and only on drier acid soils.

BILBERRY *Vaccinium myrtillus*

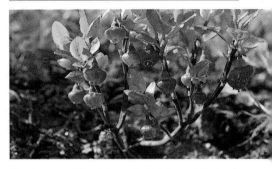

Also known as Whortleberry, Huckleberry and Blaeberry.
A hairless plant with stiff shoots and finely-toothed leaves.
The flowers are green and pinkish, and about 6 mm long. It
has edible black berries with a grape-like waxy bloom.
They are used to make jam, and yield blue and purple dye.

Size	To 60 cm
Habitat	Heaths, moorland and woodland, on acid soils. From lowland to the tops of the mountains.
Range	Found throughout, except most of the English Midlands and East Anglia.
Flowers	April-June
Similar species	Cowberry, *Vaccinium vitis-idaea*, closely related. Evergreen glossy leaves, bigger pink flowers and red, edible fruits. Mainly in Scotland and mountainous N.

SEA-LAVENDER FAMILY

COMMON SEA-LAVENDER *Limonium vulgare*

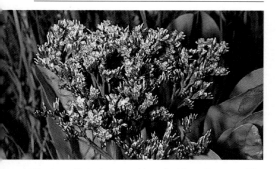

Has large, fleshy leaves and branched flowering stems. The flattish **flowerheads** are made up of many small flowers (each 6-8 mm long) and are a beautiful shade of pale purple. When dried the flowers keep their colour well, and are often used in dried flower arrangements.

Size To 35 cm
Habitat Saltmarshes and coastal mud
Range Coasts of Britain, but absent from most of Scotland, and absent from Ireland.
Flowers July-October

THRIFT *Armeria maritima*

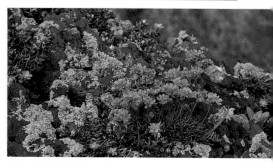

Also called Sea Pink. A favourite seaside plant with heads of pretty pink flowers, 8-9 mm across, growing up on tall, leafless stalks out of a cushion of narrow leaves.

Size	To 30 cm
Habitat	Saltmarshes, seaside pastures, cliffs and rocks. Also on mountains, particularly in Scotland.
Range	Throughout
Flowers	April-October

PRIMROSE *Primula vulgaris*

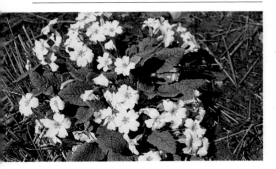

One of the best known spring flowers, with pretty, pale yellow flowers, with darker orange centres, each about 3 cm across. Several flowers emerge singly from the centre of a **rosette** of leaves. Leaves are oval with rather wrinkled edges. Sometimes crosses with Cowslip (p.131) to produce spectacular hybrids with clusters of large flowers at the top of the flower-stalk.

Size	To 10 cm
Habitat	Woodland, under hedges, on railway banks and sometimes in grassland.
Range	Common throughout, but local in S and central Ireland (sometimes common where it does occur).
Flowers	December-May

COWSLIP *Primula veris*

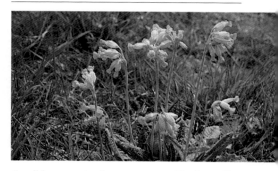

A well-known spring-flowering species. The deep yellow flowers are 10-15 mm across and grow in nodding clusters on tall stalks. The leaves are oval with rather wrinkled edges, like those of the Primrose (p.130), but narrow more abruptly into stalk. Tea made from the flowers is said to be good for insomnia, nervous tension and headaches.

Size To 20 cm
Habitat Meadows, pastures, grassy banks and roadsides.
Range Locally common throughout, but has disappeared from some areas with the removal of grassland. Rarer in W and N Scotland, N Ireland, and coasts of S Ireland.
Flowers April-May

YELLOW PIMPERNEL *Lysimachia nemorum*

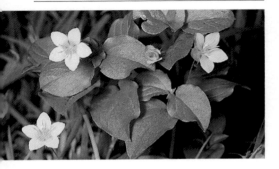

A low-growing, hairless plant with oval, pointed leaves. The yellow flowers with five **corolla lobes** are star-shaped and measure up to 12 mm across. There is a darker yellow spot at the centre of each flower.

Size	To 40 cm long
Habitat	Woods, shady hedges
Range	Throughout, although rare in parts of East Anglia
Flowers	May-September

CREEPING JENNY *Lysimachia nummularia*

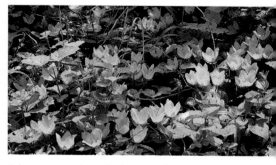

A low-growing plant which creeps along the ground.
Resembles Yellow Pimpernel (p.132), but its yellow flowers
are more cup-shaped and bigger (15-25 mm across), and its
leaves rounded, rather than pointed.

Size Only a few cm high, but creeps for 60 cm.
Habitat Hedges, grassy banks; often planted as a garden
flower and escapes.
Range Commonest in England and Wales, N to S
Scotland. Absent from central and N Scotland.
Scattered in Ireland, mainly in N.
Flowers June-August

YELLOW LOOSESTRIFE *Lysimachia vulgaris*

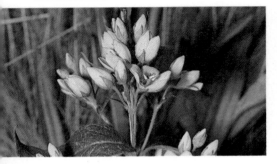

A much taller plant than Yellow Pimpernel (p.132) and Creeping Jenny (p.133), with upright growth. The flowers are bright yellow, about 15 mm across, and are clustered together on flowering **spikes**. The narrow leaves are arranged in opposite pairs or in **whorls** around the stem.

Size	To 1.5 m
Habitat	River banks, fens, marshes, lake sides
Range	Scattered throughout, but not in N and NW Scotland
Flowers	July-August

CHICKWEED WINTERGREEN *Trientalis europaea*

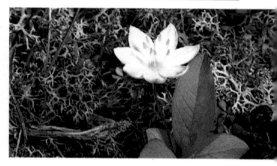

A slender plant with a **whorl** of oval leaves and a single star-shaped white flower, usually with seven petals. The flower is 15-18 mm across and grows at the end of a thin stalk about 5 cm tall.

Size	To 25 cm
Habitat	Pine woods, mossy grassland and bogs
Range	Mainly Scotland, but also S to Derbyshire and Suffolk (rare)
Flowers	June-July

SCARLET PIMPERNEL *Anagallis arvensis*

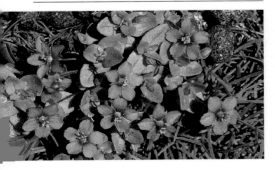

Also called Shepherd's Weatherglass because the flowers close up in bad weather. A widespread plant with pretty red flowers. It is hairless and has square stems and oval leaves. The five-petalled, red or pink (rarely blue) flowers are up to 14 mm across.

Size	To 30 cm
Habitat	An arable weed, usually near cultivated land; also on dunes.
Range	Throughout, but only scattered and mainly coastal in Scotland.
Flowers	June-August
Similar species	Bog Pimpernel, *Anagallis tenella*, is related; delicate and creeping; flowers pale pink (June-August) and leaves round. Boggy places, commonest in W.

SEA MILKWORT *Glaux maritima*

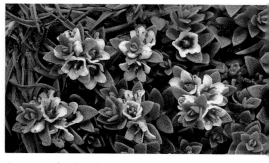

A creeping, hairless plant with fleshy, mostly opposite, leaves. There are no petals, but the **calyx** is coloured and forms the flower. The flowers are pink or pinkish-white, and about 5 mm across.

Size	To 30 cm
Habitat	Saltmarsh, coastal grassland, coastal rocks; some inland sites on salty soils.
Range	Around all coasts
Flowers	June-August

COMMON CENTAURY *Centaurium erythraea*

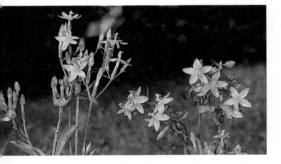

The pink flowers (each 10-15 mm across) grow together in rather flat-topped clusters. The oval leaves at the base of the plant form a **rosette**. Used in herbal medicine to treat anaemia, rheumatism and gout.

Size To 50 cm
Habitat Dunes, dry grassland
Range Throughout, but mainly coastal in Scotland and absent from N Scotland.
Flowers June-October

YELLOW-WORT *Blackstonia perfoliata*

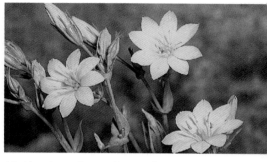

A hairless plant with pairs of opposite leaves joined around the stem. The flowers are clustered, rather like those of Common Centaury (p.138), but in this case they are bright yellow. Each flower has 8 petals and is about 8-15 mm long.

Size To 45 cm
Habitat Dunes and chalk and limestone grassland
Range Mainly S and central England, N and S coasts of Wales, central Ireland.
Flowers June-October

AUTUMN GENTIAN *Gentianella amarella*

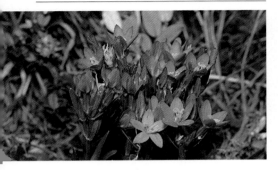

Also known as Felwort, this is our most common gentian. The flowers are long (12-18 mm) and tube-like, opening out at the top into five lobes. They do not appear until late summer or autumn, and are usually dull purple (sometimes white). The leaves are **lanceolate** and pointed.

Size	To 25 cm
Habitat	Chalk and limestone grassland, dunes
Range	Throughout, but rare in most of W Scotland and N Ireland
Flowers	August-October
Similar species	Field Gentian, *Gentianella campestris*, similar but 4-lobed flowers bluish-lilac (white), July-October. Dunes and grassland, mainly Scotland and Lake District. N and W Ireland

BOGBEAN *Menyanthes trifoliata*

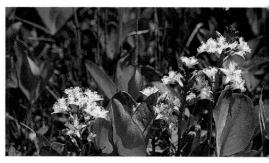

Unmistakable, with its large, rather shiny leaves each with three leaflets, rather like those of beans (hence the name). The flowers grow together on a single stalk and are pink on the outside and white inside. Each flower is about 15 mm across and has five lobes with fringed edges. Extracts of bogbean are used to treat indigestion.

Size	To 40 cm
Habitat	Bogs, fens, pond and lake edges; usually in acid water.
Range	Throughout, but commonest in N and W
Flowers	May-June

HOUND'S-TONGUE *Cynoglossum officinale*

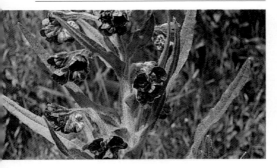

An upright plant with rather tough stems. Its long, hairy leaves resemble dogs' tongues – hence its name. The flowers are small (5-6 mm across) and maroon, growing clustered together. The leaves are **lanceolate** and when crushed have a sharp, unpleasant smell. Later in the season these are replaced by hooked fruits which cling to animal fur or clothing.

Size	To 1 m
Habitat	Grassy areas on dry soils, dunes
Range	Mainly lowland England and Wales. Absent from most of Ireland and Scotland, except parts of S and E coasts.
Flowers	June-August

COMMON COMFREY *Symphytum officinale*

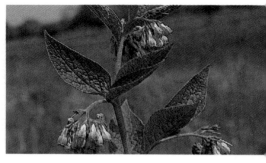

This tall, hairy plant is characteristic of river banks. It has drooping clusters of pale yellow (sometimes purplish or pink) flowers, each about 12-18 mm long. Folknames such as Boneset, Knitbone and Bruisewort tell of long medicinal use for this herb – its juice promotes the growth of connective tissue and bone. The photograph above shows the similar Russian Comfrey, *Symphytum x uplandicum*, the most common roadside comfrey, with purple-violet or red-pink flowers and rough hairs.

Size To 1.2 m
Habitat River and stream banks, wet ditches, fens and marshes
Range Throughout
Flowers May-September

COMMON FORGET-ME-NOT *Myosotis arvensis*

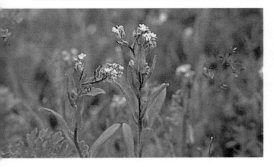

Also known as Field Forget-me-not. Our most common forget-me-not, it has very small, bright blue flowers (to about 5 mm across).The leaves are **lanceolate** and both stem and leaves have spreading hairs.

Size	To 30 cm
Habitat	Fields, woodland edge, roadsides, waste ground, dunes
Range	Throughout
Flowers	April-September
Similar species	Wood Forget-me-not, *Myosotis sylvatica*, similar but larger flowers (about 8mm). Damp woods, also common garden-escape. Mainly central and E England and S Scotland. May-September.

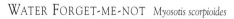

WATER FORGET-ME-NOT *Myosotis scorpioides*

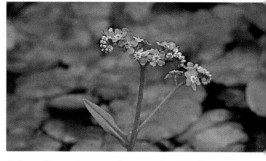

A large-flowered species (compared to the Common Forget-me-not p.144) of wet places. The flowers are about 8 mm across. The lower leaves are up to 7 cm long and oblong or **lanceolate**. The upper leaves are narrower.

Size To 45 cm
Habitat Banks of rivers, streams and ponds
Range Throughout
Flowers May-September

VIPER'S BUGLOSS *Echium vulgare*

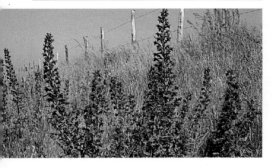

A very handsome plant when in full flower, with its tall **spikes** of vivid blue flowers (pink in bud). Each flower is 10-20 mm long. The deep flowers are particularly attractive to bees, butterflies and moths. The fruits are said to look like a viper's head, hence the name.

Size	To 1 m
Habitat	Light, mostly sandy soils, dunes or coastal cliffs
Range	Scattered throughout, but absent from most of N and NW Scotland, and only along the E coast of Ireland.
Flowers	June-September

HEDGE BINDWEED *Calystegia sepium*

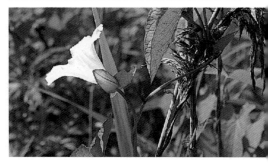

The smaller flowered of the two large bindweeds (see also Large Bindweed, p.148). Like the other bindweeds, the flowers are large and funnel-shaped, in this case pure white (occasionally pink), and up to 7 cm long. Climbs by twining around other plants or fences. The leaves are up to 15 cm long and heart-shaped.

Size	To 3 m
Habitat	Fens, wet woodland, hedges; also a garden weed.
Range	Throughout, mainly in lowlands
Flowers	July-September

LARGE BINDWEED *Calystegia silvatica*

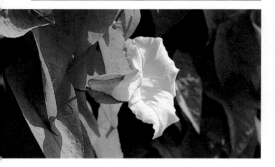

An introduction from SE Europe, via gardens. Like Hedge Bindweed (p.147), but has even bigger white (occasionally pink), funnel-shaped flowers up to 9 cm long. The 2 **bracts** (special leaves) at the flower-base are swollen, and hide the **calyx**. Climbs up stems and twigs of other plants by twining. The leaves are large and heart-shaped.

Size	To 3 m
Habitat	Waste ground, hedges and fences, gardens
Range	Throughout, especially in England and Wales
Flowers	July-September

Sea Bindweed   *Calystegia soldanella*

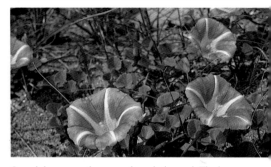

Spreads by means of **runners** through the sand. The leaves are rounded and rather heart-shaped. The flowers are pink with five pale stripes, and about 5 cm long.

Size	To 60 cm long (low-growing)
Habitat	Sandy or shingly coasts, dunes
Range	All around coasts, but rarer in NE, and absent from N and E Scotland
Flowers	June-August

FIELD BINDWEED *Convolvulus arvensis*

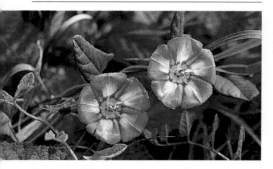

The leaves of this bindweed are shaped like a spear-head.
The flowers are small (to about 2 cm long) and white, or
pink with pale stripes. They are strongly scented and
attract many insects as a result. Spreads quickly by
underground stems.

Size To 75 cm, but often low-growing (creeps over the
ground rather than growing upwards).

Habitat Hedges, farmland, roadsides; also a persistent
garden weed with deep, underground stems.

Range Throughout England and Wales, but rarer in
Scotland; widespread in Ireland.

Flowers June-September

WOODY NIGHTSHADE   *Solanum dulcamara*

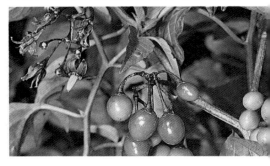

Also known as Bittersweet as the dried stems, used in medicine, taste bitter but sweeten with age. The most common wild nightshade, with distinctive flowers (15 mm), the purple petals surrounding yellow **anthers**. The fruits are poisonous, oval berries, turning from green, to yellow, to red when ripe. The leaves are either oval and pointed, or have a large lobe at the end and two smaller side lobes.

Size To 2 m (scrambles rather than climbs)
Habitat Hedges, woods, waste ground, shingle beaches.
Range Throughout, mainly lowlands; rather rare in N and W Scotland.
Flowers June-September

BLACK NIGHTSHADE *Solanum nigrum*

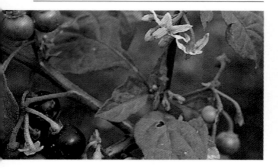

In general shape and size, Black Nightshade resembles the Potato, which belongs to the same family. The flowers are white with yellow anthers, and about 5 mm across. The fruits turn from green to black when ripe, and are poisonous. The leaves are oval and pointed, to about 6 cm long.

Size	To 60 cm
Habitat	A weed of gardens and waste ground
Range	Lowland England and Wales, most common in the S and E.
Flowers	July–September

DEADLY NIGHTSHADE *Atropa belladonna*

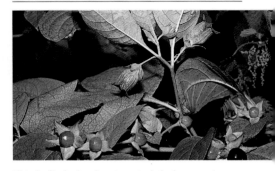

This deadly, bushy plant is particularly dangerous because its ripe berries, shiny, black and cherry-sized, look so attractive, but are in fact very poisonous. The purple flowers droop and are 2.5-3 cm long, the leaves oval, pointed and up to 20 cm. The name *belladonna* comes from the practice, once common in Italy, of using an extract of the berry to enlarge the pupil of the eye, thus enhancing beauty (*bella* = 'beautiful', *donna* = 'woman'). An extract, atropine, is still used today to enlarge the pupil in eye examinations.

Size	To 1.3 m
Habitat	Light woods, scrub, hedges on chalky soils; also sometimes around old buildings.
Range	Scattered, mainly central and E England
Flowers	June-September

HENBANE *Hyoscyamus niger*

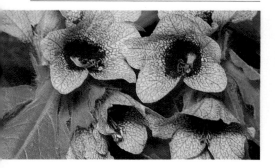

A tall plant with large, felty, oval leaves. The flowers, which develop in a cluster at the top of the plant, are yellow, with purple veins. Each is 2-3 cm across. Like Deadly Nightshade (p.153), Henbane is a very poisonous plant, but does not have attractive berries.

Size   To 80 cm
Habitat Waste ground, farmyards, old habitations, sandy soils near the coast. The seeds live for a long time in the ground, and germinate if the soil is disturbed.
Range   Scattered, mainly in S and E Britain
Flowers June-August

GREAT MULLEIN *Verbascum thapsus*

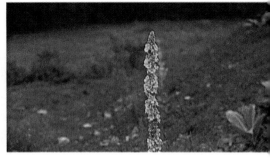

Also called Aaron's Rod, because of its straight, staff-like growth. It is a tall plant, covered in soft woolly hairs, with large, oval leaves forming a **rosette** at its base. A single, leafy flowering stem rises up from the centre, bearing a **spike** of yellow flowers, each flower 15-35 mm across. Used as a herbal remedy for coughs and asthma.

Size	To 2 m
Habitat	Banks, roadsides and waste ground on light soils. Likes warm, sunny spots.
Range	Throughout, but rarer in N and W Scotland
Flowers	June-August
Similar species	Dark Mullein, *Verbascum nigrum*, smaller, less hairy, leaves heart-shaped. S and E England.

COMMON TOADFLAX *Linaria vulgaris*

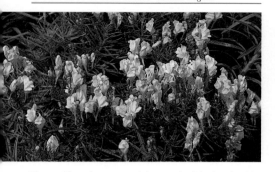

The toadflaxes have unusual flowers which look rather like Snapdragons. Each flower has an upper and a lower lip. The lower lip is divided into three lobes and closes over the mouth of the flower. This species has narrow leaves, up to 8 cm long, which grow in **whorls** around the stem. The flowers are bright yellow and orange, each 2-3 cm long, with a straight **spur**.

Size To 80 cm
Habitat Roadsides, grassy banks, hedges and waste land
Range Throughout, but rare in N and W Scotland, and only scattered in Ireland
Flowers July-October

IVY-LEAVED TOADFLAX *Cymbalaria muralis*

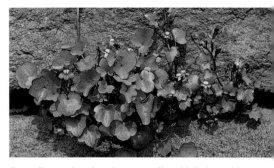

Originally a garden plant, but now well established in wild habitats as well, particularly in the cracks of walls in towns and houses. Also found rooted in crevices and trailing over rocks. The flowers are lilac coloured, 10-15 mm across, and the leaves are shaped like Ivy leaves.

Size	To 80 cm (trailing)
Habitat	Walls, rocks
Range	Throughout, but rare in N and NW Scotland
Flowers	May-September

FOXGLOVE *Digitalis purpurea*

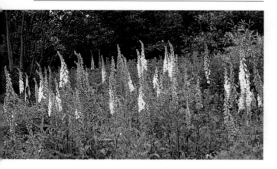

A well-known and easily recognized wild flower. The tall flower **spike** has up to 80 tube-shaped individual flowers, each up to 5 cm long. The flowers are usually pink, more rarely white. The leaves are oval and pointed, measuring up to 30 cm long. Foxgloves are a source of drugs for the treatment of heart disorders.

Size To 1.5 m
Habitat Woodland clearings, heaths, rocky outcrops, on acid soils
Range Throughout, but rather rare in the East Anglian fenland and chalky areas of SE England.
Flowers June-September

GERMANDER SPEEDWELL *Veronica chamaedrys*

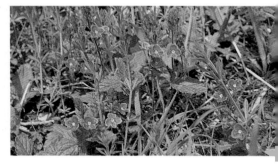

One of the largest of the common speedwells. The flowers are bright blue with a white centre, and about 10 mm across. The leaves are hairy and heart-shaped, with serrated edges.

Size	To 25 cm
Habitat	Woodland, hedges, banks and grassland
Range	Throughout
Flowers	March-July

HEATH SPEEDWELL *Veronica officinalis*

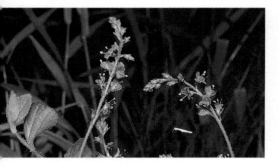

A creeping plant with hairy stems which root at intervals as they spread out along the ground. The long-stalked flowering heads grow upright from the low-growing stems. The heads are made up of between 15 and 25 lilac flowers, each about 8 mm across. Its leaves are oval and hairy, with shallow teeth.

Size	To 15 cm
Habitat	Heaths, dry grassland and open woods
Range	Throughout
Flowers	May-August

COMMON FIELD SPEEDWELL *Veronica persica*

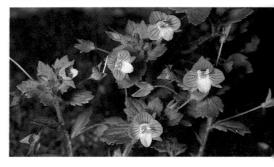

A common weed of cultivated fields, introduced in the 1820s from Asia. It has straggly growth and rather triangular leaves. The flowers are bright blue and 8-12 mm across, with a pale lower lip formed by the lower lobe of the **corolla**.

Size	To 10 cm
Habitat	Cultivated areas
Range	Throughout, but rarer in N and W Scotland
Flowers	January-December

SLENDER SPEEDWELL *Veronica filiformis*

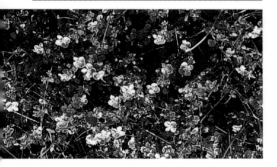

This slender, creeping species was introduced and is now common, especially in lawns where its abundant flowers can form pale blue patches in spring. The lilac-blue flowers, 8-10 mm across, grow on very thin stems. The leaves are small, to 10 mm, and rounded. Any broken piece of this plant can root, so it continues to grow well in lawns even when mown regularly.

Size	To 5 cm
Habitat	Lawns, gardens, grass verges and grazed meadows
Range	Scattered throughout
Flowers	March-July

Ivy-leaved Speedwell *Veronica hederifolia*

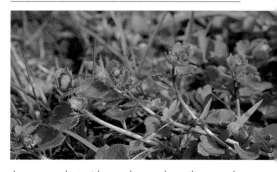

A common plant with a weak, straggly, trailing growth.
The leaves are ivy-shaped and hairy. The flowers are small,
4-5 mm across, and pale blue or white.

Size	To 10 cm
Habitat	A weed of cultivated and waste ground
Range	Throughout England, Wales and S and E Scotland. Rare in N and W Scotland, scattered and local in Ireland.
Flowers	March-August

THYME-LEAVED SPEEDWELL *Veronica serpyllifolia*

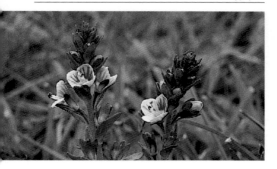

A common speedwell with oblong, shiny leaves. The flowering stems end in a cluster of small pale blue or white flowers with darker veins. Each flower is between 6-8 mm across.

Size To 10 cm
Habitat Grassland, heaths, waste and cultivated land
Range Throughout
Flowers April-September

WALL SPEEDWELL *Veronica arvensis*

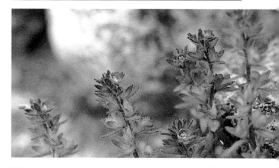

This is an upright growing, small speedwell, covered in soft hairs. The tiny blue flowers are about 3 mm across and grow in the leaf **axils**. The leaves are triangular and toothed.

Size To 20 cm (variable and often much smaller)
Habitat Cultivated and waste land, heaths, rock-ledges, wall tops
Range Throughout
Flowers March-October

BROOKLIME *Veronica beccabunga*

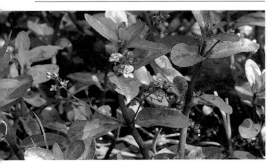

This speedwell grows in shallow water or in wet marshy ground. It has long, oval, rather fleshy leaves. Paired flowering stalks grow up from the leaf **axils**, and each has a cluster of flowers at the end. The flowers are blue and up to 7 mm across. The leaves can be eaten in salads as an alternative to watercress.

Size	To 60 cm
Habitat	Wet meadows, streams, ponds
Range	Throughout, but rare in NW Scotland
Flowers	May-September

LOUSEWORT *Pedicularis sylvatica*

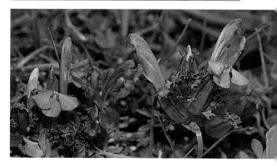

The pink flowers of Lousewort are up to 2.5 cm long and very striking, with their overarching hoods. They grow up from a mat of deeply divided leaves. Like several other members of this family, this plant is semi-parasitic: it lives attached to the roots of other species from which it gains part of its food.

Size To 20 cm
Habitat Damp heaths, moors, bogs
Range Throughout, but commoner in the N and W
Flowers April-July
Similar species Marsh Lousewort, *Pedicularis palustris*, more upright, flowers 2 cm and purplish-pink. Wet heaths and bogs, May-September.

YELLOW-RATTLE *Rhinanthus minor*

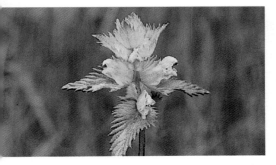

An upright plant with tough stems and opposite, rather long, toothed leaves. The flowers are large (to 15 mm long) and yellow and have an inflated **calyx**. When ripe, the seeds rattle inside the fruiting head – hence the name. It is a semi-parasite, attaching itself to the roots of other species from which it gains nourishment.

Size	To 50 cm
Habitat	Damp grassland, particularly permanent pasture and hay meadows
Range	Throughout
Flowers	May-September

COMMON COW-WHEAT *Melampyrum pratense*

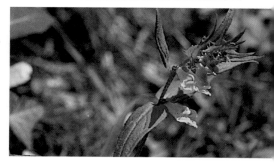

This plant has long, thin leaves, and yellow flowers which grow in pairs up the stems. The flowers, each about 10-18 mm long, all face the same way. It is semi-parasitic, living attached to the roots of other plants from which it gains food.

Size	To 60 cm
Habitat	Dry woodland, heaths
Range	Scattered throughout, but rarer in E England and in much of Ireland.
Flowers	May-October

EYEBRIGHT *Euphrasia*

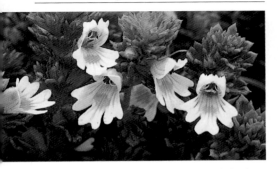

There are many species of eyebright, all difficult to distinguish. But as a group they are quite easy to recognize. They are small plants, usually growing amongst grasses, with bright flowers clustered together on leafy stems. Each flower is about 5-10 mm long, lilac or white, often with a yellow centre. The leaves are oval and toothed; opposite towards the base of the plant, but alternate towards the top. Eyebrights are used to treat sore eyes, nasal congestion and catarrh. They are semi-parasites, living attached to the roots of other plants in order to gain nourishment.

Size	To 40 cm
Habitat	Grassland, heaths, woodland edges
Range	Scattered throughout
Flowers	June-September

RED BARTSIA *Odontites verna*

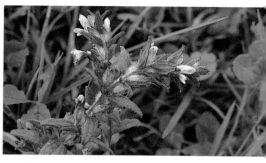

A rather scruffy-looking, hairy plant with a purplish tinge to its stems and leaves. The purple-pink flowers (each 8-10 mm long) grow bent over to one side. A semi-parasite living attached to the roots of other plants for food.

Size	To 50 cm
Habitat	Cultivated fields, waste places, open grassland
Range	Throughout, but mainly coastal in central and N Scotland
Flowers	June-August

WATER MINT *Mentha aquatica*

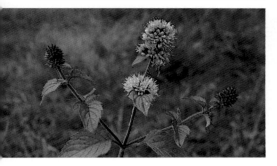

Like nearly all mints, this species smells strongly when crushed. The lilac flowers are clumped in rounded heads near the tops of the stems. The stems have a distinct red colour, and the leaves are oval, toothed and rather shiny. Mints contain aromatic oils useful for treating indigestion and colds.

Size To 1 m
Habitat Marshes, wet woods, stream sides, ponds
Range Throughout
Flowers July-October

CORN MINT *Mentha arvensis*

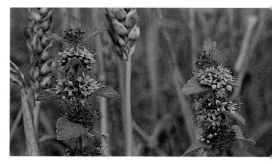

Unlike Water Mint (p.172), this is a plant of rather drier places. It is also unusual in not having an obvious minty smell. The flowers (each 3-4 mm long) grow in clusters lower down the stem rather than at the top. The leaves are rather long, and hairy on both sides.

Size	To 60 cm
Habitat	Arable fields, woodland clearings, waste ground
Range	Throughout, but mainly in lowlands
Flowers	May-October
Similar species	Spearmint, *Mentha spicata*, commonest garden mint, also wild. Leaves pointed and hairless. Flowers lilac, pink or white spikes July-September. Scattered, rare in Ireland.

GYPSYWORT *Lycopus europaeus*

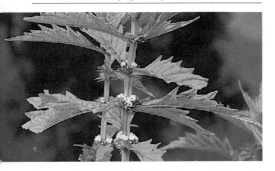

Once used as a source of black dye by gypsies, hence the name. Looks like a large mint (see Water Mint and Corn Mint p.172 and p.173), but is almost unscented, and the leaf margins are deeply cut. The flowers are small (about 3 mm across) and white.

Size To 1 m
Habitat River banks, ditches, marshes
Range Throughout lowlands, but more scattered in N Scotland and Ireland.
Flowers June-September

MARJORAM *Origanum vulgare*

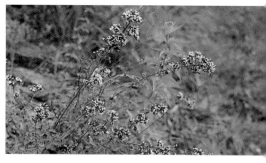

Marjoram is a well-known herb, with a strongly aromatic smell and taste, used as a flavouring for food. It has a bushy growth and a purple tinge to the stem and leaves. The leaves are rather small, to 4 cm long. The flowers are 6-8 mm long, grow in a mint-like cluster (see p.172), and are a pretty shade of pink-purple.

Size	To 80 cm
Habitat	Dry grassland, hedges and scrub, on chalky soils
Range	Scattered throughout, but absent from central, N and W Scotland. Commonest in the south.
Flowers	July-September

WILD BASIL *Clinopodium vulgare*

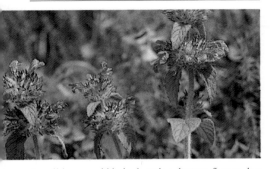

A well-known edible herb with a distinct flavour, but much less strongly aromatic than Marjoram (p.175) (although cultivated basil has a strong flavour). Resembles Marjoram, but lacks the purple tinge to the stem and leaves. Both stem and leaves are covered in soft hairs. The leaves are long and oval. The pink-purple flowers, each 12-20 mm long, are clustered at the tip of the stem and at the leaf bases lower down.

Size	To 80 cm
Habitat	Hedges, scrub on dry, chalky soils
Range	Mainly lowland England and Wales; Scattered in S and E Scotland, and SE Ireland.
Flowers	July-September

BASIL THYME *Acinos arvensis*

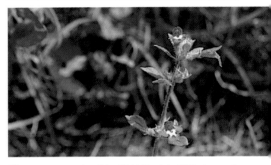

This species is rather like Wild Basil (p.176), but with smaller leaves (to 15 mm), and larger than Wild Thyme (p.178). Basil Thyme has violet or blue flowers, with white markings, each to about 10 mm long. The flowers are not as tightly clustered as those of Wild Basil. Despite its name it is not often used as a herb.

Size	To 20 cm
Habitat	Arable fields, dry grassland, on chalky soils
Range	Mainly S and SE England; scattered in SE Ireland
Flowers	May-September

WILD THYME *Thymus praecox*

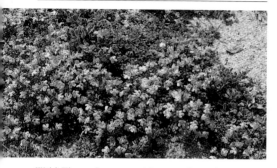

Wild Thyme has a mat-like growth, with creeping, branched, rather woody stems and small oval leaves. The leaves give off the characteristic thyme smell when crushed. The small pink-purple (sometimes white) flowers are about 3-4 mm long and clustered at the tips of the flowering shoots. A well-known herb for flavouring food, although the species usually used in cooking is the stronger Garden Thyme *Thymus vulgaris*, a native of South Europe, often grown here in gardens.

Size To 7 cm
Habitat Dry grassland, heaths, dunes, rocks
Range Throughout
Flowers May-August

Hedge Woundwort *Stachys sylvatica*

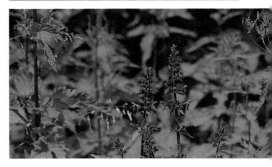

A common, large plant of shady hedgerows, with a
characteristic unpleasant smell when crushed. The leaves
are large and tapering, with distinctly toothed edges. The
flowers are deep reddish-pink and 12-18 mm long.
Woundworts have a medicinal reputation – bruised leaves
are said to stop bleeding and promote healing.

Size	To 1 m
Habitat	Woods, shady hedges
Range	Throughout
Flowers	July-August
Similar species	Betony, *Stachys officinalis*, close relation with spikes of purple-red flowers and a **rosette** of heart-shaped, toothed leaves. Woods, grassland, heath, England and Wales, June-September.

MINT FAMILY

BLACK HOREHOUND *Ballota nigra*

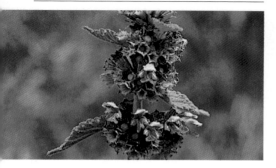

Looks rather like a tall, straggly dead-nettle (see Red Dead-nettle p.182), but the leaves have a nasty smell. The **flowerheads** are tight clusters of purple flowers, each about 15 mm long. The leaves have coarse teeth and are oval or heart-shaped.

Size To 1 m
Habitat Hedges, banks, roadsides
Range Mainly England and Wales, in lowland sites
Flowers June-October

WHITE DEAD-NETTLE *Lamium album*

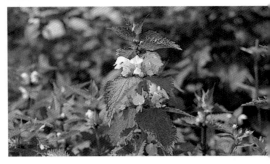

One of our prettiest wild flowers, with loose clusters of large white, hooded flowers, each 20-25 mm long. The lip of the flower provides a convenient landing stage for visiting bees and other insects which pollinate the flowers. The toothed leaves are heart-shaped and pointed. Dead-nettles are so called because their leaves look like nettle leaves, but they do not sting.

Size To 60 cm
Habitat Hedges, waste land and arable fields, gardens
Range Throughout, but rare or local in N and W and probably only introduced in Ireland.
Flowers May-December

RED DEAD-NETTLE *Lamium purpureum*

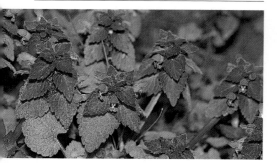

Like White Dead-nettle (p.181), another common dead-nettle, but a smaller plant with pink-purple flowers, each 10-15 mm long. The leaves are hairy and heart-shaped, with rounded teeth; they resemble those of Stinging Nettle, but do not sting.

Size	To 45 cm
Habitat	Waste land and arable fields, gardens
Range	Throughout
Flowers	March-October
Similar species	Henbit Dead-nettle, *Lamium amplexicaule*, similar flowers, but leaves joined in pairs round stem. E Britain.

YELLOW ARCHANGEL *Lamiastrum galeobdolon*

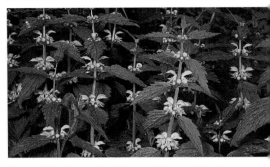

A beautiful, tall woodland plant, which spreads by long, leafy **runners**. The leaves are like those of dead-nettles (p.181) and the flowers large (17-20 mm long), hooded and bright yellow.

Size	To 60 cm
Habitat	Damp woods on heavier soils
Range	Mainly England and Wales
Flowers	May-June

SKULLCAP *Scutellaria galericulata*

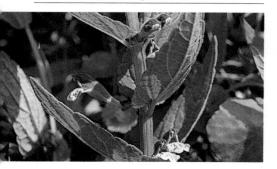

This fine plant has large, hooded flowers which are blue-violet in colour and up to 2 cm long. They grow in pairs, pointing in the same direction. The leaves are oval and slightly toothed.

Size To 50 cm
Habitat Streamsides, fens, water meadows
Range Throughout, but rare in E Scotland, and in Ireland
Flowers June-September
Similar species Lesser Skullcap, *Scutellaria minor*, smaller, pink-purple flowers, 6-10 mm. Mainly S and W, usually wet, acid soils. July-October.

WOOD SAGE *Teucrium scorodonia*

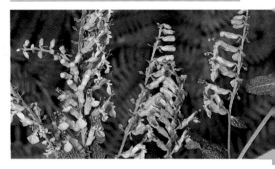

A pale green, hairy plant with oval, rather crinkled leaves and an aromatic smell. The yellow-green flowers grow in tall **spikes**. The individual flowers are quite small, about 8 mm long, with a five-lobed lip. It is not closely related to edible sage, and not used as a herb.

Size	To 30 cm
Habitat	Woods, heaths, grassland, dunes, rocks; on rather dry, acid soils.
Range	Throughout, but rather rare in parts of central England and E Anglia and in central Ireland.
Flowers	July-September

SELFHEAL *Prunella vulgaris*

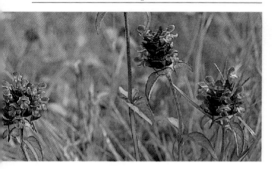

Selfheal has dense **spikes** of violet flowers on short erect stems. Each flower is 10-15 mm long, and hooded. The leaves are oval and stalked. The common name indicates traditional herbal use, and indeed this flower contains oils used for treating sore throats.

Size	To 30 cm
Habitat	Grassland, clearings in woods, lawns
Range	Throughout
Flowers	June-September

BUGLE *Ajuga reptans*

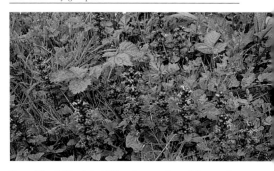

Resembles Selfheal (p.186) with its **spikes** of flowers, but the flowers are blue, about 15 mm long and not hooded. The base leaves are stalked and 50 mm long, the unstalked stem leaves grow in pairs. Spreads freely by long, leafy **runners**.

Size	To 40 cm
Habitat	Wet woods, meadows
Range	Throughout
Flowers	May-July

GROUND-IVY *Glechoma hederacea*

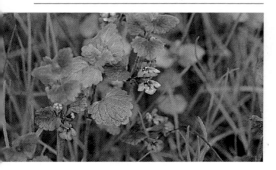

A small, common plant, with long, creeping and rooting stems and rounded, hairy leaves. The flowers (each 15-20 mm long) are violet and have purple spots on the lower lip.

Size To 30 cm, but often smaller
Habitat Grassland, waste places, woods
Range Throughout, but rare in N Scotland
Flowers March-May

HAREBELL   *Campanula rotundifolia*

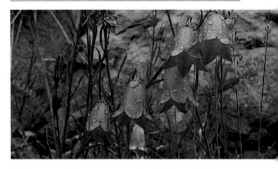

Perhaps one of the most attractive of all our wild flowers. The delicate, pale blue (rarely white) bell-shaped flowers, each 12-20 mm long, are held up on thin stalks and sway in the breeze. The leaves at the base of the plant are rounded and long-stalked, while the stem leaves are thin and grass-like. This species is called Bluebell in Scotland, (see also the species more usually called Bluebell on p.242).

Size	To 50 cm
Habitat	Dry grassland, heaths
Range	Throughout; in Ireland only common in N and W
Flowers	July-September

CLUSTERED BELLFLOWER   *Campanula glomerata*

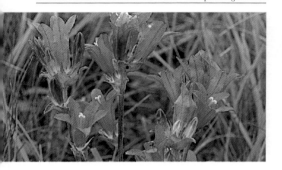

This species has short, hairy stems with clusters of purple-blue (rarely white) bell-shaped flowers, held upright. Each flower is up to 2.5 cm long. The base leaves are oval and long-stalked, the stem leaves unstalked.

Size	To 20 cm
Habitat	Chalk grassland
Range	Mainly S and E England, also SE Scotland. Absent from Ireland.
Flowers	May-September

GIANT BELLFLOWER   *Campanula latifolia*

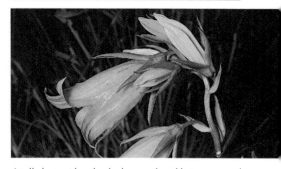

A tall plant, with rather bushy growth and hairy stems and leaves. The flowers, which are purplish-blue (sometimes white), are big (to about 4 cm long). The base leaves are up to 20 cm long and the stem leaves narrow to a sharp point.

Size	To 1.2 m
Habitat	Woods, hedges, banks
Range	Scattered in Britain, mainly in the N of England, rare in S England and N Scotland.
Flowers	July-August

NETTLE-LEAVED BELLFLOWER *Campanula trachelium*

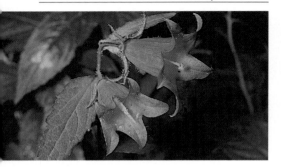

A slightly smaller version of Giant Bellflower (p.191). The flowers are smaller (to about 3.5 cm) and slightly darker blue. The base leaves are about 10 cm long; the stem leaves resemble those of the Stinging Nettle in shape.

Size To 1 m

Habitat Woods and hedges

Range Mainly S and E England and E Wales. A few localities in SE Ireland. Not in N England or Scotland.

Flowers July-September

SHEEP'S-BIT *Jasione montana*

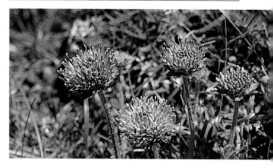

This species has small heads of tightly packed, bright blue flowers. The **flowerheads** are about 3.5 cm across, the individual flowers 5 mm long. The leaves are small and oblong, and all grow low down on the stem. It looks a bit like a scabious (see Field Scabious, p.205 and Small Scabious, p.206). Sometimes found on sheep pasture, hence the common name.

Size	To 50 cm
Habitat	Dry, acid grassland and dunes
Range	Mainly in the W of Britain and Ireland
Flowers	June-August

GOOSEGRASS *Galium aparine*

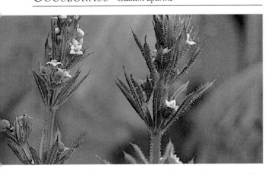

A familiar garden weed which climbs up other plants. The flowers are greenish-white and tiny, only about 2 mm across. The leaves are long and narrow, with prickly edges. Also called Cleavers because of the clinging, hooked hairs which cover the leaves and stem, and because of the round hooked fruits which stick to clothing and animal fur. Used to make natural shampoo and deodorants. Also used in medicine to treat urinary infections and skin disease.

Size	To 1.2 m
Habitat	Found in many habitats, from woodland and gardens, to shingle and waste ground.
Range	Throughout
Flowers	June-August

HEDGE BEDSTRAW *Galium mollugo*

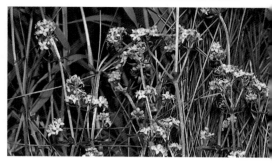

A large bedstraw common in hedgerows, it has clusters of small, white flowers, each flower about 3 mm across. The stems are smooth and the leaves grow in **whorls** of 6-8. Climbs up shrubs in hedges and wood margins. The fruits are hairless, not clinging like those of Goosegrass (p.194).

Size	To 1.2 m
Habitat	Hedges, scrub, woodland
Range	Scattered throughout, but commonest in lowland England. Only scattered in Scotland and Ireland.
Flowers	July-August

LADY'S BEDSTRAW *Galium verum*

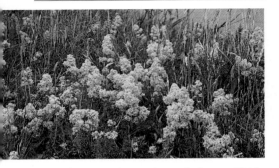

A very distinctive plant, with its soft clusters of bright yellow flowers which smell of hay. Each flower is 2-3 mm across. The leaves are narrow, dark green and in **whorls** of 8-12. Often creeps amongst grasses, sending up tall flowering stems in summer. Its fruits are smooth and about 1.5 mm across.

Size	To 1 m
Habitat	Grassland, hedges, dunes
Range	Throughout
Flowers	July-August

WOODRUFF   *Galium odoratum*

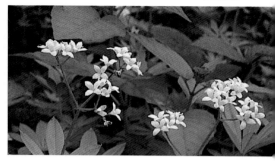

A woodland plant with relatively large flowers for a bedstraw, each about 6 mm across. The flowers are white and grow in clusters at the top of the stems. The leaves grow in **whorls** of 6-8 and have prickly edges. The fruits are 3 mm across and have hooked bristles. The whole plant is sweet-scented, especially when dried. Sometimes called Sweet Woodruff.

Size	To 45 cm
Habitat	Woods on damp, usually chalky, soils
Range	Throughout
Flowers	May-June

BEDSTRAW FAMILY

CROSSWORT *Galium cruciata*

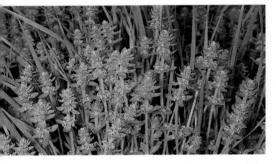

The entire plant of Crosswort is yellow-green and the flowers, each 2-3 mm across, are yellow. The leaves are oval and arranged in **whorls** of four like a cross, hence the name.

Size To 70 cm
Habitat Meadows, open woods, scrub, usually on chalky soils
Range England and Wales, to S Scotland. Not in Ireland.
Flowers May-June

HEATH BEDSTRAW *Galium saxatile*

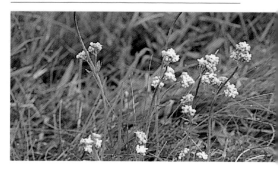

This species has a low, mat-like growth, and leaves arranged in **whorls** of 6-8. The flowering stems grow up and end in a cluster of white flowers, each about 3 mm across.

Size To 25 cm
Habitat Heaths, acid grassland, moorland
Range Throughout
Flowers June-August

COMMON MARSH BEDSTRAW *Galium palustre*

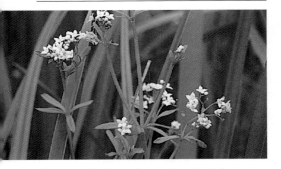

The common bedstraw of wet habitats, it climbs up stems of other marsh plants such as reeds and rushes. The short, blunt leaves grow in **whorls** of 4-6. The white flowers are about 3-4 mm across.

Size To 35 cm

Habitat Marshes, fens and ditches; usually in places which dry out each season.

Range Throughout

Flowers June-August

Similar species Fen Bedstraw, *Galium uliginosum*, similar, but sharp-pointed leaves (whorls of 6-8) and smaller flowers. Not N Scotland or N Ireland. July-August.

HONEYSUCKLE *Lonicera periclymenum*

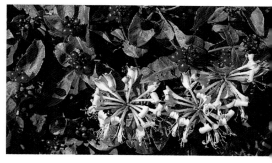

A very well known woody climber, with large heads of yellow and pink flowers. Each flower is shaped like a tube, with the **stamens** sticking out, and is 3-5 cm long. The flowers are sweet-smelling and attract moths and other insects. The fruits are bright red berries.

Size	To 6 m
Habitat	Woods, hedges, scrub, also on rocks in some places
Range	Throughout
Flowers	June-September

COMMON VALERIAN *Valeriana officinalis*

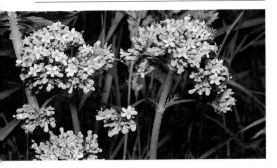

A tall plant with opposite, **pinnate** leaves and heads of small, pale pink flowers, each 2.5-5 mm long. One of its alternative names is All-heal, and it is indeed used medicinally, to treat nervous tension, insomnia and headaches.

Size	To 1.5 m
Habitat	Rough grassland, scrub, wood margins and fens
Range	Throughout
Flowers	June-August
Similar species	Marsh Valerian, *Valeriana dioica*, smaller, with long **runners** and lobed stem leaves. Flowers pink. Fens, marshes and bogs. March-June.

RED VALERIAN *Centranthus ruber*

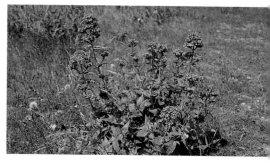

An escape from gardens now very widely spread in the wild. A beautiful plant, with opposite, rather shiny, oval, pointed leaves and clusters of red, sometimes pink or white, flowers. Each flower is 8-10 mm long. Very attractive to butterflies, bees and other insects.

Size To 80 cm

Habitat Gardens, walls, cliffs, railway embankments

Range Scattered, commonest in S and W. Absent from most of Scotland, and in Ireland mainly in S and E.

Flowers June-August

TEASEL *Dipsacus fullonum*

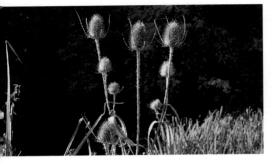

A tall, tough-stemmed, prickly plant with oval, spiny **flowerheads**, about 8 cm long. The individual tiny **florets** are purple (sometimes white). Often used in displays of 'everlasting' dried flowers. The seeds, which develop inside the flowerheads, attract birds such as Goldfinches.

Size To 2 m
Habitat Riverbanks, roadsides, hedges, waste land
Range Common in England, mainly in S. Absent from much of Scotland and Ireland.
Flowers July-August

FIELD SCABIOUS *Knautia arvensis*

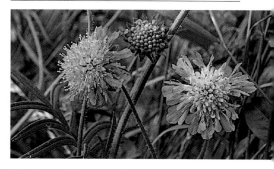

A handsome plant with rather flat heads of bluish-lilac flowers, each **flowerhead** about 3-4 cm across. The stems are rough and hairy. The stem leaves are deeply cut and the base leaves spoon-shaped.

Size	To 1 m
Habitat	Dry grassland, banks
Range	Throughout, but rare in N Scotland and NW Ireland
Flowers	July-September

SMALL SCABIOUS *Scabiosa columbaria*

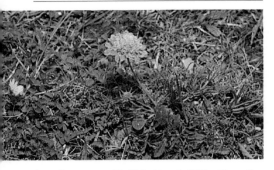

A smaller version of Field Scabious (p.205), with smaller, bluish-violet **flowerheads** about 15-30 mm across. When fruiting, the honeycomb texture of the oval heads is very distinctive. The base leaves are spoon-shaped and the stem leaves **pinnate**.

Size	To 70 cm
Habitat	Dry chalk grassland, banks
Range	Throughout England and Wales, but not in Ireland, nor most of Scotland
Flowers	July-August

DEVIL'S-BIT SCABIOUS *Succisa pratensis*

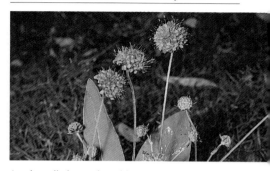

A rather tall plant with oval leaves at its base and narrow stem-leaves. The flowering heads are rounded and about 20-25 mm across. The flowers are a deeper purple-blue than those of Field Scabious (p.205) and Small Scabious (p.206). Its strange name comes from the short root, which looks as though it has been bitten off. The Devil is supposed to have bitten it off to destroy its medicinal properties.

Size To 1 m
Habitat Marshes, fens, damp meadows and wet woodland
Range Throughout
Flowers June-October

DAISY *Bellis perennis*

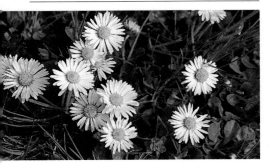

One of our most familiar wild flowers, adorning many a lawn, and common everywhere. The bright 'flowers', like those of all composites, are actually made up of a collection of tiny individual flowers (**florets**). The centre of the 'flower' is yellow and is surrounded by white 'petals' (**ray florets**). The leaves are rounded and grow in **rosettes**.

Size	To 12 cm
Habitat	Short grassland, lawns, waste ground
Range	Throughout
Flowers	January-December

Yarrow   *Achillea millefolium*

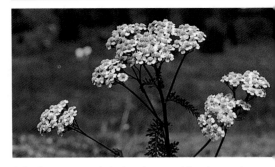

A familiar species, with feathery leaves and flat clusters of white or pinkish **flowerheads**. Each flowerhead is about 4-6 mm across. Achilles, the hero of Greek legend, is supposed to have used this plant to heal battle wounds in his troops, hence the Latin name. Herbal medicine uses Yarrow for a host of remedies, from healing wounds, to remedies for colds and fever, stomach ulcers and rheumatism.

Size	To 60 cm
Habitat	Grassland, waste land, hedges, roadsides, lawns
Range	Throughout
Flowers	June-August

PINEAPPLEWEED *Matricaria matricarioides*

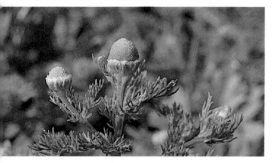

A strong smell of pineapple distinguishes this somewhat scruffy looking plant. It has rather odd-looking **flowerheads** which lack the spreading, petal-like **florets** of most members of the daisy family (see Daisy, p.208). Its leaves are finely divided, with narrow, pointed lobes. It was introduced from America in 1871, and has now spread everywhere.

Size To 30 cm
Habitat Footpaths, waste ground, roadsides, bridleways and cart tracks
Range Throughout
Flowers May-August

SCENTLESS MAYWEED *Tripleurospermum inodorum*

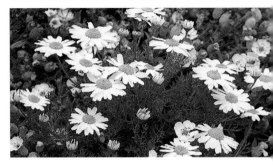

The commonest daisy-like weed of arable fields and waste ground. As its name suggests, it has no obvious scent. The daisy-like (p.208) **flowerheads** are large (to 4.5 cm across), with a flattish centre. The leaves are deeply dissected.

Size	To 60 cm
Habitat	A weed of arable fields, waste ground, footpath edges and sea shores
Range	Throughout
Flowers	July-September

CORN CHAMOMILE *Anthemis arvensis*

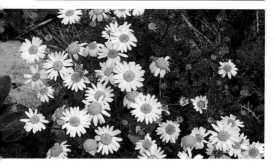

Like Scentless Mayweed (p.211), this species has large (2-3 cm across), daisy-like **flowerheads** (see p.208), but is pleasantly scented. The plant is hairy and the leaves are often woolly underneath.

Size	To 50 cm
Habitat	Arable land and waste ground, on lime-rich soils
Range	Mainly in S and E England, scattered in E Scotland
Flowers	June-July
Similar species	Stinking Chamomile, *Anthemis cotula*, related, similar, but smells unpleasant and is hairless. Arable fields on heavy soils. S and E England, July-September.

OXEYE DAISY *Leucanthemum vulgare*

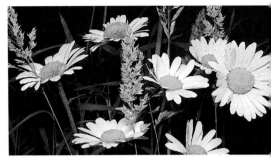

A large-flowered daisy-like plant (p.208), with flowering heads held high on long stalks. The **flowerheads** can be as large as 6 cm across. The base leaves are spoon-shaped and about 10 cm long. The stem leaves are more oblong and toothed. Also called Marguerite or Moon-daisy. An even larger form, known by the same names, is often grown in gardens and also turns up in the wild.

Size	To 70 cm
Habitat	Grassland
Range	Throughout
Flowers	June-August

TANSY *Tanacetum vulgare*

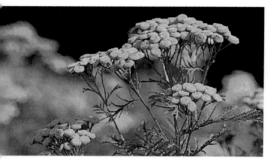

A stiff plant with deep green leaves and dark, purplish stems. The yellow **flowerheads** are tight and button-like (about 7-12 mm across), and grow in loose clusters. Tansy contains a natural insecticide – the leaves used to be strewn on floors to deter fleas. Also used in herbal medicines to treat infection by threadworms.

Size	To 1.2 m
Habitat	Waste ground, hedges, roadsides
Range	Throughout, but scattered in Ireland
Flowers	July-September

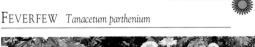

FEVERFEW   *Tanacetum parthenium*

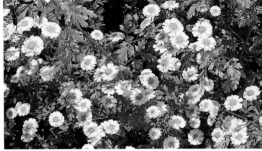

Very aromatic, with a characteristic musky smell. The leaves are a light yellow-green. The **flowerheads** each look rather like a Daisy (p.208), with a yellow centre surrounded by a ring of short 'petals' (actually special flowers or **ray florets**). As you would expect from its name, Feverfew is an effective medicinal herb. It has been proved to help relieve migraine and other headaches, as well as arthritis and asthma.

Size	To 60 cm
Habitat	Waste ground, walls, old gardens, hedges, roadsides
Range	Throughout, but rather scattered in N and W Scotland and in Ireland
Flowers	July-August

MUGWORT *Artemisia vulgaris*

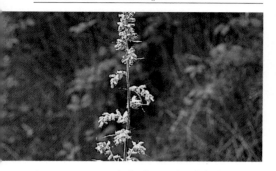

A very common roadside plant with tall, bushy growth, reddish stems and divided leaves. The **flowerheads** are very small (2-3 mm across), red-brown and inconspicuous, and are wind-pollinated. Mugwort was thought to have magic properties and was used to ward off evil spirits.

Size To 1.2 m
Habitat Waste land, roadsides, banks, hedges
Range Throughout, but mainly coastal in Scotland
Flowers July-September

HEMP AGRIMONY *Eupatorium cannabinum*

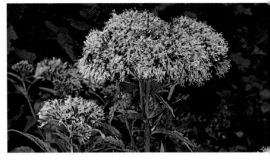

A tall, bushy plant with fluffy, pinkish clusters of **flowerheads** (each 2-5 mm across) which attract many insects, including butterflies. The leaves are toothed, divided and arranged opposite each other on the stems.

Size	To 1.5 m
Habitat	Stream sides, river banks, marshes, fens; also in damp woods
Range	Throughout lowlands, but mainly coastal in Scotland
Flowers	July-September

GOLDENROD *Solidago virgaurea*

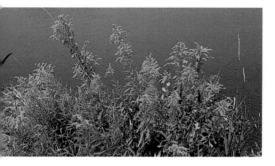

Goldenrod has tall flowering stems with **spikes** of yellow-gold **flowerheads**. Each flowerhead is about 10 mm across, with 6-12 rays. The base leaves are spoon-shaped and stalked, the stem leaves **lanceolate** and unstalked. This species is used in herbal medicine to treat urinary infection, arthritis, catarrh and diarrhoea.

Size	To 75 cm
Habitat	Dry woods, grassland, rocks, cliffs, hedges, dunes
Range	Throughout, although rarer in E and central England, and central Ireland
Flowers	July-September
Similar species	The larger Canadian Goldenrod, *Solidago canadensis,* often escapes from gardens to wasteland.

COMMON FLEABANE *Pulicaria dysenterica*

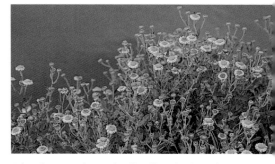

A late-flowering plant with yellow **flowerheads** to about 3 cm across, and broad, pointed leaves. This plant was burned and its smoke used to drive away fleas, hence the name.

Size	To 60 cm
Habitat	Marshes, wet meadows, ditches
Range	Throughout England, Wales and S Ireland; rarer in N and absent from most of Scotland.
Flowers	August-September

BUTTERBUR *Petasites hybridus*

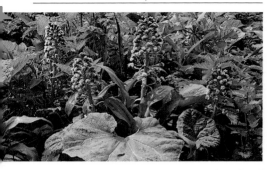

This plant has large leaves (a bit like rhubarb leaves), and is commonly seen along stream banks. The flowers, which appear before the leaves, are purplish-pink and arranged in very solid **spikes**. Each flower is 3-12 mm across. The male and female plants are separate, and female plants are rare in parts of lowland England. The leaves were once used to wrap butter, hence the common name.

Size To 80 cm
Habitat Wet meadows by streams, often under trees
Range Throughout, but rarer in central and N Scotland.
Flowers March-May

COLTSFOOT *Tussilago farfara*

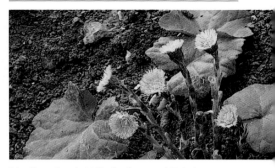

Like Butterbur (p.220), the flowers of Coltsfoot appear
before the leaves. The **flowerheads**, which are 15-35 mm
across, are rather like those of Dandelion (p.234), but bend
over as they mature. The seeds are also fluffy and
windborne. The leaves are triangular, with a heart-shaped
base. Coltsfoot has long been used as a herbal medicine for
coughs and colds.

Size To 30 cm
Habitat Waste land, arable fields, roadsides, river banks,
dunes, shingle and scree
Range Throughout
Flowers March-April

RAGWORT *Senecio jacobaea*

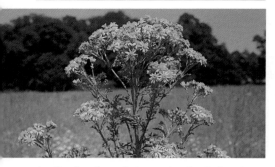

A tall, yellow-flowered plant, with rather feathery leaves. The flowering heads are arranged in a flat-topped group. Often attacked by the black and yellow caterpillars of the Cinnabar Moth, which may even kill the plant if sufficiently numerous. A serious weed of pastureland, somewhat poisonous to cattle, and also to rabbits which avoid it.

Size To 1.5 m
Habitat Pastures, waste ground, sand dunes
Range Throughout
Flowers June-October

OXFORD RAGWORT *Senecio squalidus*

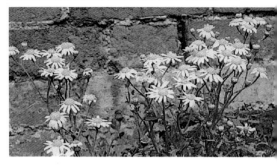

Introduced from Italy, first recorded on old walls in Oxford in 1794, and now a widespread weed. This ragwort has a bushy growth. The leaves are deeply lobed, with narrow leaflets. The **flowerheads** are bright yellow and 15-25 mm across.

Size	To 40 cm
Habitat	Old walls, waste ground, especially by railways
Range	Throughout England and Wales; rare in Ireland and Scotland
Flowers	June-December

GROUNDSEL *Senecio vulgaris*

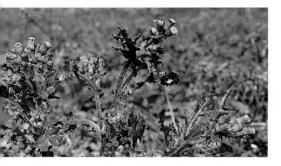

This common garden weed differs from the other ragworts (pp.222, 223) in not having any obvious **ray florets**. The yellow **flowerheads** are cylindrical, not flat like those of the Daisy (p.208), and about 4 mm across. The leaves are shiny above, with rather blunt lobes. It is a rather weak plant with succulent stems.

Size	To 45 cm
Habitat	Waste ground, arable fields, gardens
Range	Throughout
Flowers	January–December

BURDOCK *Arctium*

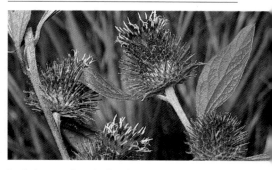

Burdocks are robust, bushy plants with large leaves and characteristic hooked fruits, or burs, which cling to animal fur or to clothing. There are several species, but they are difficult to distinguish, although the burdocks themselves are easy to recognize as a group. The large leaves are rough and heart-shaped. The **flowerheads** are rounded and develop the hooked spines when in fruit. The plant is used to add a bitter flavour to drinks (e.g. dandelion and burdock) and also in herbal medicine to treat skin disorders.

Size	To 2.5 m
Habitat	Waste places, roadsides, open woods
Range	Throughout
Flowers	July-September

DAISY FAMILY

MUSK THISTLE *Carduus nutans*

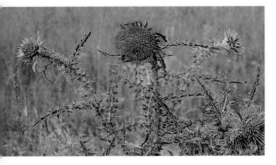

One of the prettiest thistles, with nodding purple heads of sweet-smelling flowers, the heads are 4-6 cm across. The leaves are lobed and tipped with sharp spines. The stems have spiny wings which stop well below the **flowerheads**. Beloved of bees, butterflies and other nectar feeding insects.

Size	To 1 m
Habitat	Waste places, arable fields, roadsides and rough pastures
Range	Mainly in England, Wales and SE Scotland, but not in Ireland
Flowers	May-August
Similar species	Welted Thistle, *Carduus acanthoides*, stem winged to flowerheads.Grass verges, waste land, stream banks. Common in S; rare Ireland. June-August.

CREEPING THISTLE *Cirsium arvense*

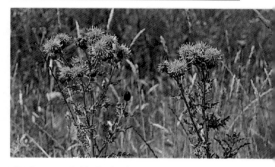

Also known as Field Thistle, this is a very common weed of fields and pastures. The dull purple flowering heads are small (to 2.5 cm) and clustered. Like most thistles, it is well protected by prickly leaves, which have triangular lobes. The stem is not winged. The plant spreads by creeping through the soil.

Size	To 1 m
Habitat	Fields, pastures, waste ground
Range	Throughout
Flowers	July-September
Similar species	Spear Thistle, *Cirsium vulgare*, similar but stem spiny and winged, red-purple **flowerheads** larger. Fields, pastures, waste ground, gardens throughout. July-October.

MARSH THISTLE *Cirsium palustre*

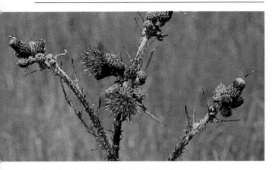

Like the Spear Thistle (p.227), this species has a spiny winged stem, but is usually taller and has smaller **flowerheads** (usually less than 2 cm across). These are dark reddish purple (rarely white). The leaves are deeply divided and spiny.

Size To 2 m
Habitat Marsh, wet grassland, wet woods
Range Throughout
Flowers July-September

COMMON KNAPWEED *Centaurea nigra*

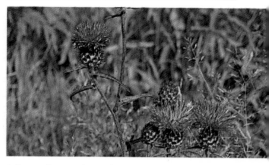

A hairy plant with tough, grooved stems and mostly undivided leaves. The **flowerheads** are tightly-packed, red-purple and about 2-4 cm across, opening from rather hard buds.

Size	To 65 cm
Habitat	Grassland, roadsides, hedges, cliffs
Range	Throughout
Flowers	June-September
Similar species	Greater Knapweed, *Centaurea scabiosa*, divided leaves and larger, decorative flowerheads. Similar habitats throughout lowlands, common in S and Ireland. July-September.

GOATSBEARD *Tragopogon pratensis*

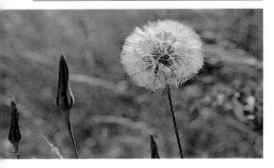

A tall, slender plant with grass-like leaves and large yellow
flowerheads (to 5 cm across) which open only in the
morning sun. This gives rise to the alternative name of
Jack-go-to-bed-at-noon. The flowers develop into hairy
fruiting heads like giant dandelion clocks, hence their
common name.

Size	To 70 cm
Habitat	Grassland, roadsides, waste ground, dunes
Range	Throughout England, but less common in W and in Wales. Scattered in Scotland and Ireland.
Flowers	June-July

SMOOTH SOW-THISTLE *Sonchus oleraceus*

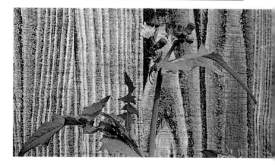

This common plant has hairless leaves without spines (unlike most sow-thistles), and pale yellow **flowerheads**, each about 2.5 cm across. Like the other sow-thistles it has milky juice in the stem and leaves.

Size	To 1.5 m
Habitat	Waste land, cultivated ground
Range	Throughout, except Scottish highlands
Flowers	June-August
Similar species	Prickly Sow-thistle, *Sonchus asper*, spiny leaves and similar sized flowerheads. Throughout, June-August.

FIELD SOW-THISTLE *Sonchus arvensis*

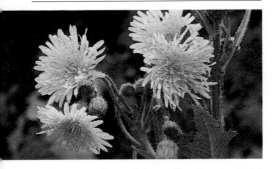

A tall, creeping plant with large yellow **flowerheads**, 4-5 cm across. The leaves have spiny, toothed edges. The upper parts of the stems often have a covering of yellowish hair. Like other sow-thistles, it has milky juice in the stem and leaves.

Size To 1.5 m
Habitat Stream sides, banks, roadsides, drift-lines of the sea and of rivers
Range Throughout, but mainly coastal in Scotland
Flowers July-October

SMOOTH HAWK'S-BEARD *Crepis capillaris*

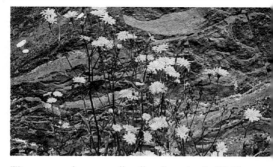

Wiry stems and many small, yellow **flowerheads** (10-15 mm across) characterize this common species. The leaves are lobed, with a triangular lobe at the end. The fruits ripen inside small conical heads.

Size To 75 cm; often smaller
Habitat Grassland, heath, walls, roadsides, waste ground
Range Throughout
Flowers June-September

DANDELION *Taraxacum*

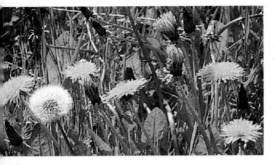

One of our most familiar flowers, with **rosettes** of long, backwardly-toothed leaves, and large yellow **flowerheads** on smooth, hollow, leafless stalks. Dandelion leaves, favourite food of pet rabbits and guinea pigs, may also be added to salads to add an extra, rather bitter flavour. The plant is also used to treat skin diseases and rheumatism.

Size	To 30 cm
Habitat	Roadsides, waste ground, lawns
Range	Throughout
Flowers	March-October

CAT'S EAR *Hypochoeris radicata*

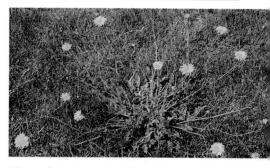

Like a tall Dandelion (p.234), with branched, leafless stems and flat yellow **flowerheads** (2.5-4 cm across). The hairy, oval leaves, which grow in a **rosette** at the base of the plant, give this species its common name – they have the texture and rough shape of a cat's ear.

Size	To 50 cm
Habitat	Meadows, pastures, roadsides, dunes
Range	Throughout
Flowers	June-September

AUTUMN HAWKBIT *Leontodon autumnalis*

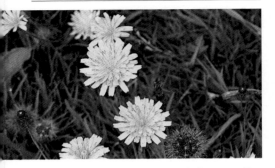

Very similar to Cat's Ear (p.235), but its yellow **flowerheads** are usually reddish underneath and smaller, 12-35 mm across. These grow on leafless, branched, slender stems. The leaves are deeply lobed, pointed and not obviously hairy, unlike those of Cat's Ear. They grow as a **rosette** at ground level.

Size	To 50 cm
Habitat	Meadows, pastures, waste ground, screes, rocks
Range	Throughout
Flowers	June-October
Similar species	Rough Hawkbit, *Leontodon hispidus*, hairy, unbranched stems, large golden flowerheads. Chalk grassland, England, Wales, S Scotland, central Ireland. June-September

HAWKWEED *Hieracium*

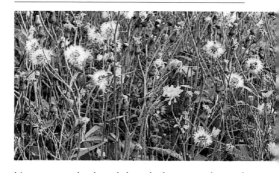

Most common hawkweeds have leafy stems and several **flowerheads**, usually light yellow and 1-4 cm across (depending on the species). There are many species, but most are difficult to identify, although they are easy to recognize as a group. Some are common on roadsides and railway banks, and generally flower in mid to late summer. The photograph shows *Hieracium vulgatum*, probably the most common hawkweed in N England and Scotland.

Size	To 1 m
Habitat	Roadsides, grassland, rocky places
Range	The group is widespread. *Hieracium vulgatum* is common in in N England and Scotland; N Ireland.
Flowers	May-August

MOUSE-EAR HAWKWEED *Hieracium pilosella*

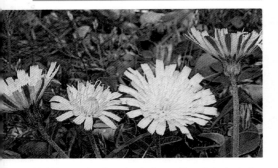

Unlike many hawkweeds which are all confusingly similar, this common species is easy to identify. It is rather low-growing, with long, white **runners** and **rosettes** of thick leaves with white felty hairs underneath. It is these leaves which give the plant its common name. The single **flowerheads** are yellow, with red streaks beneath, and 15-25 mm across.

Size	To 25 cm
Habitat	Grassland, heaths, walls, banks
Range	Throughout
Flowers	May-August

BRISTLY OXTONGUE *Picris echioides*

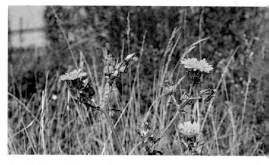

A tall plant with prickly hairs on its wavy-edged, pimply leaves, and large yellow **flowerheads** 20-25 mm across. Below each flowerhead there are five heart-shaped **bracts**.

Size	To 1 m
Habitat	Waste ground, roadsides, hedges, field margins, especially on heavy, chalky soils
Range	Mainly lowland England and Wales; rare in Scotland and Ireland
Flowers	June-October
Similar species	Hawkweed Oxtongue, *Picris hieracioides*, lacks pimples, and bracts smaller. Lowland England and Wales; rare Scotland and Ireland. July-September.

LILY-OF-THE-VALLEY *Convallaria majalis*

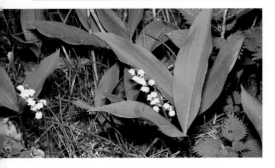

A pretty garden plant, which also grows wild in some places. It has long oval leaves, with flowering stems growing up in between. The bell-shaped, white flowers (each about 8 mm long) are sweetly scented and arranged in a loose, drooping cluster. Extracts of this plant are used in medicine to regulate the heart beat.

Size	To 20 cm
Habitat	Native in dry limestone woods; sometimes naturalized from gardens.
Range	Scattered in England and E Wales; rare in Scotland; rare in Ireland (introduced).
Flowers	May-June

RAMSONS *Allium ursinum*

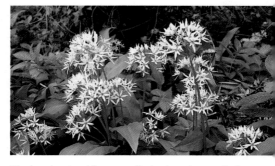

The broad, pointed leaves smell of onion when crushed, and often carpet the ground. The white clusters of star-shaped flowers, each to 2 cm across, appear in the spring. The leaves have a pleasant mild garlic flavour, hence it is also known as Wild Garlic.

Size	To 45 cm
Habitat	Damp woods, shady copses
Range	Throughout, but rare in NE Scotland, and much of S and W Ireland
Flowers	April-June

BLUEBELL *Hyacinthoides non-scripta*

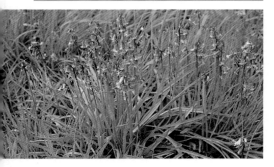

One of our most attractive wild flowers which tends to grow in large patches on the woodland floor. A Bluebell wood in May can be an unforgettable sight. The leaves are long and narrow. The flowers are bright blue (rarely white or pink) and bell-shaped and grow clustered together in groups of 4-16. The flowers are each about 2 cm long.

Size	To 50 cm
Habitat	Woods, hedges, banks
Range	Throughout, but more scattered in S Ireland
Flowers	April-June
Similar species	Garden Bluebells are usually *Hyacinthoides hispanica*, or hybrids of *H. hispanica* and *H. non-scripta*.

SPRING SQUILL *Scilla verna*

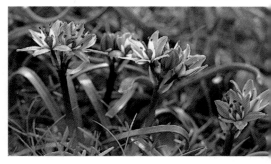

A small coastal plant with narrow, shiny, twisted leaves. The flowers are pale violet-blue and grow in clusters of 2-12 on each stem. Each flower measures about 10 mm across. The flowers face upwards and open widely, unlike those of the Bluebell (p.242).

Size	To 15 cm
Habitat	Grassland near the coast, cliff tops
Range	Mainly along N and W coasts; also on parts of E coast in Scotland and N England; and E coast of Ireland.
Flowers	April-May

WILD DAFFODIL *Narcissus pseudonarcissus*

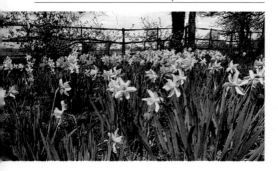

The true Wild Daffodil is small by the standards of many garden varieties, but is still large for a wildflower. It also tends to grow in groups, so can be an impressive sight. The flowers are pale yellow, with a deep yellow trumpet-like tube, and up to 6 cm long. The leaves are grey-green, long, thin and flattened.

Size To 35 cm
Habitat Damp woods and grassland
Range Commonest in the W of England; introduced to some parts of Scotland and Ireland.
Flowers March-April

SNOWDROP *Galanthus nivalis*

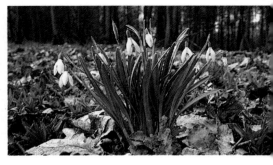

A very familiar winter-flowering plant with white nodding flowers (one flower to each flower-stalk), each about 2.5 cm long . The leaves are grey-green and long and narrow. This is another species which is often planted in gardens, and also often escapes into the wild. It may be native to parts of W England and Wales.

Size To 20 cm
Habitat Damp woods, stream banks
Range Scattered throughout Britain; rare in Ireland.
Flowers January-March

YELLOW IRIS   *Iris pseudacorus*

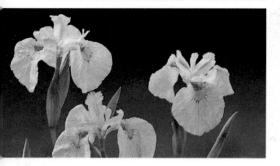

Also called Yellow Flag, this familiar tall plant has long, flattened leaves and large, bright yellow flowers, each up to 10 cm across, with 2-3 flowers on each stem. It grows from a thick **rhizome** at the base. There are many garden varieties of iris, with large flowers in many colours.

Size	To 1.5 m
Habitat	Marshes, ponds, riversides, wet woods
Range	Throughout
Flowers	May-July
Similar species	Stinking Iris, *Iris foetidissima*, similar leaves, but an unpleasant smell. Flowers smaller, dull purple. Woods, hedges, sea cliffs, mainly S England and Wales, May-July.

BEE ORCHID *Ophrys apifera*

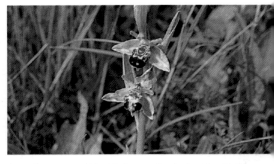

A small, pretty orchid with flowers that look rather like bumble bees, each about 2 cm across. In some parts of its range, though not in Britain, it is pollinated by bumblebees, which are fooled by the flower into trying to mate with what looks like another bee. The base leaves are oval and blunt, the stem-leaves rather pointed.

Size	To 45 cm
Habitat	Pastures, banks, chalk grassland
Range	Scattered in England, Wales and Ireland
Flowers	June-July

EARLY PURPLE ORCHID *Orchis mascula*

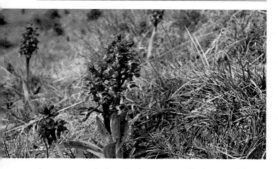

A common orchid, with glossy green, black-spotted leaves and purple flowers. The flowers grow together in a loose **spike** sticking up from the centre of a **rosette** of base leaves. Each flower is about 8-12 mm across. One of the earliest orchids to come into flower.

Size	To 60 cm
Habitat	Woods and open pastures
Range	Throughout
Flowers	April-June

MARSH ORCHIDS *Dactylorhiza*

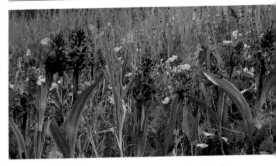

The marsh orchids are a difficult group to identify; there are several rather similar species, and hybrids with intermediate features also occur. They have pink or purple flowers, each marked by darker dots and lines, and each about 10 mm across. Unlike those of the Early Purple Orchid (p.248), the base leaves do not grow in a **rosette**, and they may be spotted or unspotted depending on the species. The species illustrated here is Southern Marsh Orchid *Dactylorhiza praetermissa*.

Size	To 60 cm
Habitat	Wet meadows, marshes, fens, wet dunes
Range	Scattered throughout
Flowers	May-August

COMMON SPOTTED ORCHID *Dactylorhiza fuchsii*

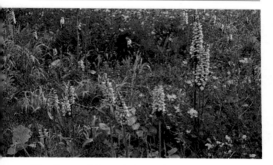

The flowers of this orchid are pale pink with darker spots or streaks, and grow in a cylindrical **spike**. Each flower is about 15 mm across. It has several broad, rather blunt-ended leaves, each marked with broad dark spots.

Size	To 60 cm
Habitat	Woods, marshes, meadows
Range	Throughout, except Scottish Highlands
Flowers	June–August
Similar species	Heath Spotted Orchid, *Dactylorhiza maculata*, similar but pyramidal spike, whitish to pale purple flowers and round spots on leaves. Woods or acid soils throughout, rare in E England. June–August.

COMMON TWAYBLADE *Listera ovata*

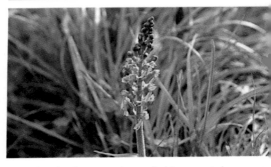

It is often hard to spot this orchid because it has inconspicuous yellow-green flowers which do not stand out against other plants. The flowers grow in a **spike** up to 25 cm tall. Best told by the twin (or tway) rounded leaves towards the base of the single stem.

Size	To 60 cm
Habitat	Wet woods, pastures, dunes
Range	Throughout, but rather rare inland in central and N Scotland
Flowers	June-July
Similar species	Lesser Twayblade, *Listera cordata*, shorter, with smaller leaves. Mountain woods and moorland, mainly in Scotland. July-September.

LORDS-AND-LADIES *Arum maculatum*

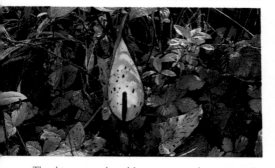

The shiny arrow-shaped leaves grow in the spring, to be followed by strange hooded flowers. Each 'flower' is a central purple rod (the **spadix**) enclosed by a translucent hood (the **spathe**). The spathe is up to 25 cm tall. It is the **spadix** which carries the tiny separate male and female flowers. The **flowerheads** have an unpleasant smell which attracts flies for pollination. Clusters of poisonous red berries develop later.

Size	To 50 cm
Habitat	Woods, hedges, banks
Range	Throughout, except central and N Scotland
Flowers	April-May

Index

[bracketed no.s] = mention only